Christianity and African Traditional Religion
Two Realities of a Different Kind

Kachere Series
P.O. Box 1037, Zomba, Malawi
kachere@globemw.net
www.sdnp.org.mw/kachereseries

Copyright 2005 Bregje de Kok

All rights reserved. No part oft this publication may be reproduced, stored in a retrieval system, or transmitted in any form or by any means, electronic, mechanical, photocopying, recording or otherwise, without prior permission from the publishers.

Published by
Kachere Series
P.O. Box 1037, Zomba, Malawi

ISBN 99908-76-17-7
Sources for the Study of Religion in Malawi no. 19

The Kachere Series is represented outside Africa by:
African Books Collective, Oxford (orders@africanbookscollective.com)
Michigan State University Press, East Lansing (msupress@msu.edu)

Layout: Olive Goba
Cover design: Olive Goba
Cover picture: Carving of a witch from Mua Mission
[EMA Catholic University of Nijmegen]

Printed by Lightning Source

Christianity and African Traditional Religion

Two Realities of a Different Kind

A cultural psychological study of the way Christian Malawians account for their involvement in African Traditional Religion

Bregje de Kok

Sources for the Study of Religion in Malawi no. 19

Kachere Series
Zomba
2005

Preface

For a long time longer than I thought I have been looking forward to write the preface of this thesis. Of course I would like to thank a few people now I've reached the end of the thesis, and thereby of my student life in Nijmegen.

To start with, I would like to thank my supervisor Cor Baerveldt, living in Canada nowadays, for his time and effort. He has been thinking hard together with me, whereas the working circumstances were not exactly ideal. Moreover, Cor has demonstrated to me- together with Paul Voestermans- how motivated cultural psychologists can be in their profession. I have become infected by their enthousiasm for cultural psychology and science in general, for which I am grateful. I'd like to thank Cor van Halen and Gerben Westerhof for reading a long story in a short time.

Rijk van Dijk of the Afrikaans Studiecentrum in Leiden is worth mentioning as he enabled me to get in touch with Joe Chakanza of the University of Malawi. Dr. Chakanza has been talking many hours with me about my research and helped me a lot. Many other people in Malawi have been supporting me during my stay as well. I would like to mention, besides Dr. Chakanza, Klaus Fiedler, Martin Ott, Mercy, Olive, Georry and Edward. Zikomo kwambiri!

Furthermore, I would like to thank my friends whom I got to know in Nijmegen –Anke, Karen, Roland, Anneke and Roel. Roel gets the credits for the picture at the front page! I have much appreciated the company of and discussions with my fellow cultural psychologists Noor, Michiel, Mieke, Bart and Philip (and Anneke of course). Many thanks to my family, who had and will have to miss me all the time I spent and will spend in Malawi. To my parents I'd like to say that I'm grateful that they supported me in choosing a study, which truly interested me.

Contents

1. Introduction
2. Analytical Perspective: Cultural Psychology and Discourse Analysis
   - 2.1 Cultural Psychology
   - 2.2 Discourse Analysis
   - 2.3 Research - question revisited

3. Methodology
   - 3.1 Data collection
   - 3.2 Respondents & Recruitment
   - 3.3 Analysis

4. Situating Discourse about ATR
   - 4.1 ATR in Malawi
   - 4.2 Prevalence of ATR in Malawi
   - 4.3 Christianity in Malawi
   - 4.4 Policy of the church: Official decrees and respondents' assertions
   - 4.5 ATR among respondents: Claims about involvement

5. Accounting Malawian Christians
   - 5.1 Problematising ATR: Identity-talk

     Intermezzo I: The questions left unanswered

   - 5.2 Problematising ATR: Pragmatic-talk

     Intermezzo II: The questions left unanswered

   - 5.3 Unproblematising ATR: Identity- and Pragmatic-talk
   - 5.3.1 Unproblematising ATR: Externalisation & Normalisation
   - 5.3.2 Unproblematising ATR: Trivialisation

     Intermezzo III: The questions left unanswered

6. Christianity and ATR-'beliefs': Of a Different order, at a Different Level
   - 6.1 Attending to ATR-'beliefs': Ambivalence, contradiction and paradox
   - 6.2 Claims of belief and claims of reality: Of a different order
   - 6.3 Christian and ATR-practices: Of a different order

       Intermezzo IV

7.   Conclusion and Discussion
7.1   Conclusion
7.2   Final comments and recommendation

List of References

Appendix A: Respondents' characteristics
Appendix B: Involvement in ATR per respondent, per practice
Appendix C: Malawi in short
Appendix D: Transcription notation
Appendix E: Interview schedule

Introduction

> 'Indeed, I do visit idols, I consult inspired men and soothsayers, but I don't leave the church of God. I am a Catholic.' (Member of Augustine's congregation, in MacMullen, 1997:148)
>
> 'They wouldn't have done so if anyone had told them it was wrong.' (Member of Augustine's congregation in reply to Augustine's rebuke of their ritual bathing, in MacMullen, 1997:146)

In European history, the ages between the fourth and eight century after Christ are known as the period of the 'Great Event', in which Christianity replaced Paganism (MacMullen, 1997). 'History doesn't like losers' says MacMullen (1997) and thus, from their omniscient perspective, historians tend to focus merely on the triumph of Christianity. However, MacMullen (1997), a historian himself, stresses that the replacement of Paganism by Christianity was neither quick nor orderly. During a long time both Paganism and Christianity were vital in the lives of people and influenced each other (MacMullen, 1997). This introduction started with quotes from members of the congregation of Augustine, one of the church fathers of the Roman-Catholic church. The quotes demonstrate the coexistence of 'Paganism' and Christianity in the first centuries after Christ. Moreover, they suggest that at least the laity did not see their dual involvement in 'Paganism' and Christianity as wrong or problematic. Apparently Christians in the first ages after Christ could openly tell to visit idols, to consult 'inspired men', and at the same time they could state in a convinced way to be Catholics.

The current study is not historical but cultural psychological. Its stage is not Europe in the fourth to eighth century, but the east-African country Malawi at the beginning of the twenty-first century. However, as will become clear in this thesis, there appear to be some striking similarities between the ways in which Europeans dealt, and contemporary Malawians deal, with the coming of Christianity in their lives. When in 1861 Christian missionaries arrived in Malawi, Malawians had their own God, their own spirits and their own religious rituals and beliefs. But the missionaries' message of the 'Good News', depicted Christianity as the superior religion, and required Malawians to forsake their indigenous religion in order to convert to Christianity (Tengatenga, 1998; Chingota, 1995). As the number of Christians has increased sharply in East-African countries in only a few decades (Schoffeleers, 1983), the mission can be said to have been successful. However, many studies of religion in Africa show that the missionaries did not always accomplish what they wanted. Sometimes they failed to ban—or even increased adherence to—certain traditional practices and beliefs. For example, Warkentin (1996) showed that in Zaire the mission did not succeed in banning the abiding of ancestral spirits among the Bira. Meyer (1994) points out that in Ghana, missionaries sustained the belief in witchcraft when they introduced the concept of the devil. The local population, not familiar with this concept, related it to an evil source they knew; witchcraft. Therefore the missionaries' warnings against the devil became a confirmation of the existence of witchcraft, although the mission condemned these beliefs as pagan and superstitious (op cit.). Also Christians in Malawi are said to continue performing indigenous religious practices, like funeral rites (Kuppen, 1992), birth-rituals (Katani, 1999), and initiation-ceremonies (Chakanza, 1998). In addition, it is said that many Malawians did not leave behind their traditional beliefs like witchcraft and ancestral spirits (Kuppen, 1992, Katani, 1999).

Thus, like once in Europe, it appears that different religious traditions are coexisting in the lives of contemporary Malawians. Intuitively it seems logical that Malawians don't forsake their own indigenous religion for a foreign religion, which has been present for less, then 150 years. In Europe it took at least four ages before 'paganism' gave way, as MacMullen (1997) pointed out. However, Malawian Christians strike as sincere Christians, and the churches of which they are devoted members predominantly disapprove of involvement in African Traditional Religion, although they have become more tolerant in the last decades (Kuppen, 1992; Chingota, 1995; Chakanza, 1998). Does this coexistence of African Traditional Religion, ATR[1] in short, and Christianity not involve a somewhat complicated combination of conflicting worldviews? Or can dual religious involvement, at least for the laity,

---

[1] Most scholars who write about religion in African countries use the concept 'African Traditional Religion', or 'ATR' in short, or similar generic names to refer to the indigenous religion. This suggests that different African countries have the same religion, which originated on this continent. Yet, undoubtedly 'ATR 'differs per African region or country. For practical reasons I will use the concept 'ATR' as well, although I do refer specifically to the indigenous religious tradition of Malawi. This is not completely an outside, 'etic' perception of Malawian practices: Christian Malawians themselves sometimes use the word 'African Traditional Religion', or its abbreviation 'ATR' when talking about their own indigenous religion.

be quite unproblematic, like the quotes of members of Augustine's congregation suggest? Might Malawian Christians admit in the same straightforward way to 'visit idols', to 'consult inspired men and soothsayers' as those Christians? Might they claim that they just need to be told that certain traditional practices are 'not done', thereby suggesting not to see problems where the church sees them?

In general, studies about religious pluralism in Africa emphasize the mutual influencing of the religious systems of ATR and Christianity. Frequently terms like 'Christianization' of African religion, 'Africanisation' of Christianity or 'syncretism' are used to refer to the fusion, which is considered to take place (Warkentin, 1996; Meyer, 1994; Dierick, 1983, Stewart & Shaw, 1994). Especially the concept 'syncretism' has obtained negative connotations as it was used to refer to littered, insincere forms of belief (Droogers, 1989; Stewart & Shaw, 1994). Moreover it is sometimes associated with lack of power of those who engage in syncretistic religious behaviour (Kiernan, 1994). These days few scholars will use 'syncretism' to refer to an inferior form of religion. But, as Stewart and Shaw (1994) point out, scholars do tend to see syncretistic religious forms as strange deviations of the 'normal' uniform religions. 'Syncretism' is frequently considered as a possible source of moral or mental, inner or outward confusion and tension (Turner, 1979, Katani 1999; Chakanza, 1998; Ott, 1999). Ott (1999) suggests that the moulding of Christian tradition, African traditional religions, modernity and global flows can have both a negative or positive outcome. The negative outcome would be 'a religious schizophrenia, whereby different systems co-exist without mediation' (1999:5). The positive outcome would be 'a successful inculturation in a situation of continuous cultural change'. 'Inculturation' is the name of the policy, which the Roman Catholic Church has promoted since 1969. This policy demands respect for the indigenous religion and seeks to incorporate, as Katani (1999) says, certain traditional beliefs and practices into the church 'without diluting the message of Christ'. Both foreign and local clergy and intellectuals regularly propose 'inculturation' as a solution for the alleged conflicting lives of Malawian Christians. However, with Meyer (1994), one can question whether such inculturation or 'syncretism from above', designed by theologians, is necessary and helpful for people at the grassroots. Meyer (1994) stresses that Africans are not just victims of western dominance. Africans fused Christianity and African Traditional religion in their own way, according to their own needs. Thus, syncretism, spontaneously enacted from below, does not have to be a sign of insincerity, nor does it have to cause, or signal, conflicts in the minds of Africans. To stimulate a fusion 'from above' might not be necessary and moreover it might not work.

In addition, the mission has influenced the ideas and practices of Africans less then both missionaries and their critics think. Pauw and Schutte (in Kiernan, 1994) point out that the coexistence of ATR and Christianity does not necessarily lead to some kind of fusion. They explain that ATR can be an *additional* source of help for Christians, without evoking feelings of severe tension or contradiction, and without Africans at the grassroots Christianizing their ATR or Africanising their Christianity. Fabian (1985) warns that people should not seek too much logical coherence in religiosity. He points out that 'where the old missionaries had given their lives to explain that Christianity and traditional religion were irreconcilable entities - a creed to which many of the anthropologists subscribed ... the younger generation of anthropologists and historians seem to delight in proving that the two are in reality one. Folk-Christianity and popular Islam have become the catchwords' (Fabian, 1985:147). According to Fabian (op cit.) one can consider the concept of syncretism as an artefact of normative interests to lump together diverse and contradictory phenomena, to make them understandable and less complicated. However, variance, discontinuity and outright contradiction in religious behaviour should be considered normal, according to Fabian.

This study will take into account Fabian's warning that one should be careful not to impose artificial uniform concepts on religious practices and beliefs. As words like syncretism or popular Christianity don't acknowledge enough that Africans do not necessarily melt two religions in one unitary system, the research topic will be phrased as the Christian Malawians' dual involvement in the religious traditions of Christianity and African Traditional Religion.

For the time being the following research question can be formulated:

How do Christian Malawians manage to be both devoted Christians, and at the same time to be involved in African Traditional Religion, which their church, on the whole, disapproves of?

Thus, the aim of this study is to gain insight into the way concrete individuals actually enact two different religions in their daily lives. Therefore, following Droogers (1983) and Fabian (1985), the focus of this study is not religious doctrines but rather on (religious) practices. This also because what can be called African traditional religion has, in contrast to Christianity, no fixed set of dogmas. It is rather a collection of practices and ideas, which especially pertain to daily life. Like the African Mbiti said: 'though Africans believe in the life after death, to live here and now is the most important concern of African religious activities and beliefs' (1969:4).

In the current study verbal interactions occurring between Christian Malawians and a western interviewer are investigated. As Fabian (1985) suggested to prevent artificially imposing order artificially 'from above', the people who are studied are given a voice, and 'religious pluralism' is studied from below.

To answer this question a qualitative study has been carried out, from a cultural psychological and discourse analytical point of view. In the next chapter the analytic perspectives of cultural psychology and discourse analysis will be explained.

2. Analytic Perspective: Cultural Psychology and Discourse Analysis

As this study is grounded in cultural psychology and discourse analysis, the relevant characteristics and assumptions of both will be explained in the next two paragraphs.

2.1 Cultural psychology

From the perspective of an *enactivist* cultural psychology, as proposed by Baerveldt & Verheggen (1998), culture is studied as 'human affair'. Baerveldt and Verheggen (1998) stress that individuals are active agents, who continuously 'enact' culture. In daily, concrete interactions people continuously tune their behaviour to each other. After recurrent interactions, members of a social group start doing things in similar ways; they greet each other in their group-specific way, laugh in the same kinds of situations and show their anger in similar ways. As it is from repetitive, consensual co-ordination of actions that culturally patterned behaviour emerges, 'culture' should be conceived as the *result* of behaviour instead of as its *cause*. Culture does not make people think, feel and act in specific cultural ways. This specific cultural psychological perspective conforms with Garfinkel, who stated already in 1969 that people are no cultural dopes who simply internalize, and act in accordance with, cultural norms (in Antaki & Widdicombe, 1999).

In an enactivist cultural psychology it is acknowledged that 'culture' is dynamic as interacting individuals continuously make and remake 'culture'. 'Culture' is continuously in the process of becoming, 'under construction'. It should be mentioned that many social scientists claim that culture is dynamic (van Binsbergen, 1981, van Binsbergen & Schoffeleers, 1985; van Dijk, 1989) However, most of them attribute changes in culture to external macro-factors, like changing power-relations or changing economic systems (van Binsbergen, 1981, 1985). In these structuralist perspectives the enacting individuals get lost.

Culturally patterned behaviour, which emerges from the tuning-process, tends to become automatic, unreflected and taken for granted. In Malawi, male friends regularly hold hands. And no Malawian will find this remarkable. However, Europeans are likely to immediately notice two men holding hands and will try to make sense of it, possibly by suggesting that the two men could be homosexual lovers. When a Malawian is asked for an explanation, it is most likely that he will explain the men's behaviour by stating that they are friends. Its automatic, unreflected and taken for granted nature makes cultural behaviour difficult to discuss and to change; cultural behaviour-patterns are persistent. It will become clear in this thesis that decades of mission-work in which the 'Good News' was brought to Africa made many Africans convert to Christianity, but did not make them to abolish their indigenous religion.

The example of the Malawian men holding hands shows that in the continuous production of social behaviour people continuously produce *meaning*. Hence, the task for cultural psychologists is not only to understand the way in which cultural patterned behaviour is produced, but also how 'meaningful worlds are produced and reproduced, sustained and disputed in actual social practices' (Baerveldt, 1999:25).

People tend to see especially foreign, 'exotic' people as 'cultural dopes'. Especially foreigners' behaviour is too easily explained away by putting forward their culture (Voestermans & Baerveldt 2000; van Dijk, 1984). The enactivist perspective on culture makes clear that *all* behaviour—our own just as well as that of 'strangers'—is cultural. Moreover, *all* behaviour is at the same time both cultural and personal. For, also the most peculiar, typical cultural habits are the result of enacting individuals who co-ordinate their behaviour in such a way that their acts can be observed *as to* follow cultural rules. But, as will be clear by now, such observed cultural rules should not be put forward as cause of the behaviour. This is making the major fallacy, which Bourdieu refers to; 'putting in the minds of people what you have in your own mind in order to understand what they are doing' (Bourdieu, 1990:80). Thus, when trying to gain insight in the reproduction of patterns in behaviour, pertaining to dual religious involvement in Malawi, it will not do to describe the 'Malawian People' in terms of their 'Malawian Culture'. Referring to general cultural characteristics like Africans' 'respect for elderly', their 'capability for religious bilocation' (Dierick, 1983) or the fact that they are religiously mobile' (Schoffeleers, 1983) will not provide insight in the way Christians in Africa manage to be involved in two religious traditions. Nor will anthropological studies, which attribute functions to traditional religious practices, and thereby 'explain' their persistence, provide satisfactory insights. It might be, as van Binsbergen (1981) suggests, that Zambians' witchcraft beliefs are grounded in the egalitarian nature of their society and lack of juridical means to solve conflicts. It might be that the Chewa in Malawi keep on performing Nyau-rituals because this serves as a 'safety-valve', whereby people can get rid of social tensions at fixed times (Kuppen, 1992). However, such structural-functionalistic explanations will not provide a psychological understanding of the way in which Malawians manage to be involved in two religious traditions in social live. Behavioural functions, which observers make up, following their own academic logic, cannot be assumed to be of relevance for the acting individuals themselves. Human behaviour is not necessarily organized according to scientific logic. Unless it can be demonstrated that individuals themselves—the Malawian Christians believing in witchcraft, the Chewa still performing Nyau—attend to these 'functions' in their concrete verbal and non-verbal actions.

How exactly then, *can* insight be gained in the way in which Christian Malawians produce and reproduce, sustain and dispute a world of dual religious involvement? This will become clearer after the discourse analytic perspective has been explained.

2.2 Discourse analysis

> 'Whether as Azande diagnosticus, Western astrophysicist or bored passenger on an airport-bus, we prove that the outside world exists, and agree upon its properties, by talking about it together in the same way.' (Moerman, 1988:116)

Some forms of discourse analysis derive part of their inspiration from conversation analysis. Therefore, the starting points of conversation analysis, which are discussed below, pertain to this study's discourse analytic perspective as well.

Conversation analysts study the social organisation of talk, in order to reach systematic insight into the ways in which members of society 'do interaction' (Ten Have, 1990 d). Conversation analysts study talk from an 'action-perspective' instead of from a 'factist perspective' (Alasuutari, in Ten Have, 1999c). Talk is not studied as information-channel to mental affairs like attitudes or cognitive processes, or to events in the world out there, but as 'tool to get things done' (Potter and Wetherell, 1987:18). The focus is on how talk is designed or constructed and on what is accomplished with this design. When studying—as cultural psychologists—talk from a conversation analytical perspective the question can be posed to what kind of psychological, or interactional problems the discursive actions of conversation partners are to provide a solution.

Ten Have (1999c) points out that people continuously describe in specific ways what they themselves and other people do, want, feel, and think.

People elucidate on what they do and characterise what others do. These linguistic acts are called accounting practices (*op cit.*). In talk different people, at different moments create different 'particular versions of reality'; they account in different ways for, and thereby construct, what's the matter or what happened (Edwards, 1995). Also Moerman (1988), following Berger and Luckman, mentions a reality maintenance-function of talk, which he describes as a magical power: 'Conversation's 'magic power' ... is us talking so as to put our minds together by building a world to co-inhabit'. It will become very clear in the coming chapters how Christian Malawians account for and therein construct a specific kind of 'reality', which differs from for example a typical secular, European version of 'reality'.

Thus, conversation and discourse analysts have a social constructionist perspective on reality and meaning, according to which it is undeterminable to which extent talk reflects reality. They consider the above-mentioned factist perspective on talk as problematic. What people say—and do—is no unproblematic window on co-participants minds, or on a world 'out there' (Heritage and Atkinson, in Ten Have, 1999d). By focussing, as said before, on talk as action, as 'tool to get things done' (Potter and Wetherell, 1987:18), discourse and conversation analysts circumvent this problem.

People are not unrestricted in what they say and do in social life and in talk. There is a demand for members of a social group to account in such a way that one's actions become understandable and legitimate (Slugoski & Ginsburg, 1989; Harré, 1989). As Harré (1989:30) points out, this 'moral necessity' to account in certain ways is intrinsically social; 'I am authorised to undertake something when the judge, the committee, the king, the medical profession or all socially defined entities so decree'. For Christian Malawians, amongst others clergy, family-members, fellow-villagers and a western interviewer can be added to this 'judging audience'. Individuals talk and act on the basis of anticipated responses of such relevant 'Others', either actually present or imagined (Shotter, 1989). In social interaction people learn how to take 'Others' into account as affording different actions, as fellow members of the social order who will interpret, judge and possibly sanction utterances in a certain way (Shotter, 1989). Thus, when studying talk from a discourse analytic perspective it is taken into account that respondents are no talking questionnaires (Potter & Whetherell, 1987), and that they will not perceive the interviewer as a living tape-recorder. Interactants will continuously and actively tune into each other.

When studying interviews conversation analysts aim at explicating the membership-competencies that ordinary speakers use in participating in intelligible, socially organized, talk. Hereby the study of specific wording of people in talk is crucial as it is considered to have a constitutive function in social life and 'there just does not seem to be any other way then the painstaking analysis of detailed records to do the job' (1999d).

2. 3 Research question revisited

The outline of this study's analytical perspective has made clear that cultural psychology studies how individuals continuously create, in interaction, culturally patterned behaviour and meaningful worlds. The discourse analytic perspective adds a focus on accounts and discursive devices which members of societies use to partake in intelligible, justified talk and to create 'particular versions of reality'. In this research the way in which Christian Malawians account for involvement in both Christianity and ATR -when talking to a white female researcher- will be studied. The purpose of this research is not only to identify what kinds of accounts Christian Malawians give. It also seeks to find out what the interviewed Christian Malawians can accomplish by providing a specific description of certain actions or a certain state of affairs; what 'particular versions of reality' do they construct, what kind of interactional problems can be solved. Now more knowledge about this study's analytical perspective has been obtained, the research question can be rephrased as follows:

1. *What kind of accounts do the Christian Malawian respondents give for involvement in ATR, of either themselves or others?*
2. *What do the respondents accomplish by providing these accounts?*
3. *If they problematise or unproblematise dual involvement in ATR and Christianity, how exactly do the respondents accomplish such an (un-) problematisation?*

Charting the accounts will reveal a pattern in Malawian Christians' interactional behaviour. By investigating the discursive strategies, which Christian Malawians use in talk, this study seeks to gain insight in underlying psychological and interactional mechanisms, which generate the specific pattern of accounting-practices.

3. Methodology

As is common in qualitative, ethnographic research, this study's research methodology is characterised by 'triangulation'. Data were collected by different methods: participant observation, document-analysis and especially interviews. In this chapter these means of data-collection, the relevant characteristics of the respondents, sampling-method and method of analysis will be shortly discussed.

3.1 Data collection

Participant observation

From October 1999 until April 2000 fieldwork has been carried out in and around Zomba, a town in southern Malawi. I - a female white researcher- wrote down observations which I found striking and which pertained in some way to people's ATR or Christian practices. I also wrote down personal feelings which accompanied certain observations in order to become – as much as possible- aware of the influence of subjective interests and assumptions which might influence observations and interpretations. In addition, I attended and observed classes of the first year course 'Introduction to Religious Studies' at the University of Malawi. This provided both background information about ATR, and insights in how young contemporary Malawian Christians talk about and make sense of traditional religious practices and beliefs.

Document analysis

Articles in newspapers and magazines and ethnographic essays about ATR practices of first year university students were studied. Like the participant observation, this document analysis provided some insight into the relevance of certain practices and beliefs for contemporary Malawians, and into the way people talk about – judge, make sense of - Malawian Christians' ATR-involvement.

Unstructured and semi-structured interviews

The researcher had several more or less spontaneous conversations about the research topic with lay Malawians, foreign missionaries, and both foreign and local clergy. They were written down as soon as possible after the conversation.

Besides these unstructured interviews, semi-structured interviews were carried out with key-persons and respondents. Key-persons like clergy, theologians and missionaries were approached to gain background information about ATR in Malawi and the policy of the church. Respondents were Christian Malawians, both laymen and clergy. For the semi-structured interviews an interview-schedule was used (see appendix D) which was adjusted several times during the six-month stay in Malawi. In this way it became more field-oriented instead of theory-based. On average, the interviews took two hours and they were all recorded on tape. In general, respondents were first asked about their actions in so-called 'crisis-situations' in life; puberty, illness, death, birth, and drought. Thereafter they were asked to which extent they were familiar with and involved in traditional religious practices and beliefs related to these events. Respondents were also asked about their Christian practices and beliefs and about their knowledge and opinion about the church-policy with regard to ATR practices and beliefs. Furthermore, respondents were confronted with involvement in ATR of either themselves or frequently hypothetical Christian acquaintances. For example, respondents were asked whether they thought that devoted Christians could be involved in ATR. In the last part of the interviews respondents were asked whether they felt the need for 'inculturation': the incorporation of ATR or tradition in general in their Christian faith.

3.2 Respondents and Recruitment

9 male and 5 female respondents were interviewed about ATR and Christianity in their daily lives. Two women, 'J' and 'L' were interviewed together. All respondents spoke English reasonably well. 4 respondents were Roman-Catholics, 9 belonged to the Church of Central Africa Presbyterian (CCAP) and 1 to the New Apostolic Church. Two were reverends in the CCAP, and one was a deacon in this church. The focus was on CCAP and Roman-Catholic members because these denominations form the biggest part of the Christian population in Malawi. In addition, the CCAP and Roman Catholic Church were said to have a different stance with regard to ATR and dual involvement. Therefore, it was interesting to have both groups represented. The respondents belonged to different ethnicities, amongst others to the Yao, Tumbuka, Nyanja, Tonga, and Lomwe. One respondent

had finished her primary school; the others had at least passed their JCE, which means they had completed at least half of their secondary school. The age of the respondents ranged from 16 to 64. Respondents lived in or around Zomba or Domasi in southern Malawi. Most of them were born in relatively rural areas.

Selection-criteria for respondents were whether they were Christian and had enough English fluency to be able to have a normal conversation. To make sure that women and men, Roman Catholics and CCAP, young and old people were represented, sometimes the researcher selected respondents on the base of these criteria as well. The interviewer knew some of the respondents before the interview. Others were selected via 'snowball sampling'; the researcher asked some respondents whether they could introduce her to people who spoke English quite well and were Christians. In appendix A information is provided about personal characteristics per respondent.

3.3 Analysis

The interviews were all recorded on tape and for the largest part they were transcribed verbatim. Hereby also characteristics of speech like pauses, intonation, laughing, overlap of speech, and the like have been transcribed. For discourse analysis, where talk is considered as 'tool to get things done' (Potter & Whetherell, 1987), these characteristics are at least as meaningful as the words which are used themselves. In appendix D a list of transcription-notations can be found.

The transcribed interviews were divided into extracts and codes were administered to make the large data set more manageable. Initially these codes were based on the literal content of the extracts. Later they reflected more abstract thematic similarities.. Coding was not considered as analysis as such but as aid for analysis: it made it easier to trace extracts, which were interesting for detailed discourse-analysis. On the basis of this detailed analysis, different types of accounts could be identified and categorized. The categorization is based on the identification of similar discursive structures, which were discerned after closely examining many different interview-extracts of different interviews. Thus, the categorization is the researcher's ordering, but one which is grounded in and does justice to the concrete verbal interactions in which the respondents create their own order.

In order to show what Malawian Christians do in their talk about ATR, many transcribed extracts can be found in this thesis. Providing several interview-extracts per account would make it easier for readers themselves to discover patterns in the discursive structures. However, in order not to turn this thesis into a never-ending story, sometimes only one concrete interview-extract or even only summaries of interview data will be discussed. For the same reason the collection of Malawian Christians' accounts which is discussed in this thesis is far from exhaustive.

4. Situating Discourse about ATR

> 'In all conversation, people are living their lives, performing their roles, enacting their culture ... To understand what the moves mean requires (or recalls) cultural knowledge.' (Moerman, 1988, p. 22)

Moerman (1988) proposes a type of conversation analysis, which is culturally contextualized. He stresses that historical background, cultural contexts and cultural meanings of speech events should be taken into account when studying talk. From this perspective, if one wants to investigate accounting-practices of people who belong to foreign cultures, one will have to obtain at least some ethnographic knowledge before one can grasp what people are doing in their talk. Moerman explains' I take on the task as ethnographer to show how these things [cultural meanings and categories] work in this society, and as a conversation analyst that and how they were involved and used in hat very moment of talk' (1988:7). Therefore, to be able to understand Malawian Christians' 'moves' in conversation, some ethnographic information will be provided in this chapter. The different ATR-practices and beliefs, which are 'alive' in contemporary Malawi, are described. Furthermore, the prevalence of ATR and Christianity in contemporary Malawi among different strata of the population is discussed, as is the policy concerning ATR of the CCAP and Roman-Catholic church in Malawi.

To understand patterns in the discourse about ATR it might be helpful to have access to some information about the society in which Malawians live. For this reason, some historical and demographic data about Malawi can be found in appendix C.

The descriptions in this chapter are mainly based on: participant observations; essays about ATR of first year theology students; informal discussions with Malawians. The background-information provided is not only an analyst's tool but also a participants' resource: in the interviews respondents can frequently be observed to orient to the information, which is provided in this chapter.

4.1 ATR in Malawi

What do people –both non-Malawian 'outsiders' and Malawians themselves- actually refer to when talking about 'African Traditional Religion' in contemporary Malawi? A short –ideal typical- ethnographic description will be given of the main ATR-aspects, which are relevant in contemporary Malawi. These ATR-practices and beliefs appear to be especially related to so-called 'crisis-moments' in life: birth, death, puberty and illness (Meyer, 1994; Chakanza, personal communication, Jan 2000.)

Ancestral Spirits

In African Traditional Religion, ancestral spirits are considered to be mediums between God and the human world. They are considered to interfere much in daily life, in contrast to God, who is considered to be a rather aloof supreme being. Since the coming of Christianity, belief in ancestral spirits seems to have declined. Yet, many Malawians will still declare that ancestral spirits *exist* and are *real*. Ancestral spirits, who might become offended in case certain customs or taboos are violated, are feared. Offended spirits might come to haunt you – spirit possession is regularly reported- and cause misfortunes, like disease or drought. Correctly performing rituals and executing orders of spirits who appeared in dreams can appease ancestral spirits.

Witchcraft

In Malawi certain people – witches - are considered to possess supernatural powers with which they can influence other people's fortune in life, mostly in a negative sense. Witchcraft is considered to cause illness, death or other misfortunes. Especially people leading lives which other people envy -for example because they are highly educated or have good jobs- are thought to run the risk of being bewitched. Moreover they might be suspected of using witchcraft themselves; how did they become so prosperous otherwise?

Witches are mostly women, although they can be men as well. They are said to make use of instruments when executing their witchcraft. If typical 'witch-utensils' are found in someone's house, this is considered to prove that the suspect is indeed a witch. Another feature of witches is their ability to fly, in so-called 'fly-baskets'. During their flights, they are invisible to normal human beings. There are certain practices, which are said to protect against witchcraft, like birth-rituals, funeral-rites and traditional healing. Traditional healers can either revenge or bewitch persons who evoked witchcraft in the first place, or they can provide protective herbs or amulets. Also Christianity can fulfill a protective function; it is sometimes said that the almighty God can protect one from witches.

The fear of some university-students to go back to their home-villages because they might either be bewitched or accused of witchcraft, illustrates the way witchcraft works in Malawi. Witchcraft appears to be an omnipresent, irrefutable reality in Malawi. Many, diverse people, ranging from illiterate villagers to university-students and –staff, are convinced that witches *exist* and that witchcraft is *real*. Certain Malawian-experts, both local and foreign, claim that 'witchcraft is a force which destroys everything in Malawi' (Ott, personal communication). Some consider witchcraft a factor, which impedes the already slow development of Malawi; people might be less ambitious if they know prosperity will make people envious and therefore inclined to bewitch you.

Initiation rites

Many Malawians, both Christians and non-Christians, send their children to initiation, although undoubtedly this happens less often than in the past. Initiation is a 'rite of passage', which marks one of the important transitions in life. Initiations are considered to contribute to, or even to be necessary for, the transition of girls and boys into adult women or men. Usually boys and girls attend initiation –separately- around the onset of puberty. Some ethnic groups have two or three different initiations at different ages. In those cases children will attend their first initiation when they are only five or six years old. Duration of initiation varies from a couple of days to approximately a month. Certain Malawian ethnic-groups have individual, others communal, initiation- ceremonies.[2] The latter take place in a fixed period of the year.

Initiations have an educative function; initiates are taught about sexuality, inter-sexual relationships and gender-roles. Lessons are not merely theoretical; adults sometimes have intercourse in front of the children, and it is said that, in certain initiations girls are obliged to have intercourse with an instructor at the end of the initiation. This practice however, seems to have become almost, if not completely, extinct.

Especially the boys' initiations are said to be quite harsh and violent. Occasionally boys are beaten up at the beginning of the ceremony, which would prepare them for hardships they will endure in life. Boys of one or

---

[2] Malawians themselves do not always call individual initiations initiation. One can indeed doubt what the difference is between individual 'initiations' and pedagogic conversations about growing up and puberty which many parents in western countries have with their adolescent children.

two ethnic-groups in Malawi are circumcised. The Yao for example are known for this practice. Girls are not circumcised anymore in Malawi.

Initiations have an exclusive, secretive character. Often they take place somewhere in 'the bush'. Only the initiates themselves and their instructors, usually respected elderly are allowed to be present. Non-initiated are not allowed to know what is told at initiation. It is common to convey knowledge at initiations in the form of songs and riddles the meaning of which is only clear for those who have undergone 'chinamwali'. It is said that after initiation many initiates separate themselves from their non-initiated peers. They pretend to be of more importance due to the special knowledge they just obtained. Some girls are said to prefer to start a relationship with initiated boys. Those who are not initiated can feel shy when starting a sexual relationship with an initiated person, afraid not to be able to meet expectations due to lack of sexual knowledge and skills taught at initiation.

Not all ethnic groups still have initiations these days, and when they do, it is more frequently for girls. Initiation, and more specifically sexual education, would be especially important for girls, who some call the 'guardians of life' (J. Chakanza, December 1999, personal communication).

Nyau or 'Gule Wamkulu'

The Nyau or 'Gule Wamkulu' -'Great Dance' in English- is a traditional society, which belongs to the ethnic group of the Chewa. Chewa can become Nyau after initiation in this 'Secret Society'. Among the main features of this group are the masked figures, which show up during different rituals. Only male members of this Secret Society have the right to wear the masks. These men are said to turn into a spirit the moment they put on a mask. Each masked figure has its own symbolic meaning. Masks differ to some extent per village, and they change over time. For example, since the mission came to Malawi some biblical figures like Maria and Josef show up in Nyau-rituals and since Muluzi became president there are masks, which represent him.

The Nyau are notorious for the violent behaviour of their 'spirits', who are said to steal, molest and even kill. Nowadays these Nyau-practices seem to have been enervated, although Nyau are still very controversial and feared.

Traditional healing

Like in other African countries with poor health standards and poor quantity and quality of western health services, traditional healing is a common practice in Malawi. The least controversial form of traditional healing is self-medication, when people administer herbs to themselves in order to cure their health-problems. There are also professional traditional healers in Malawi. They can be subdivided into herbalists on the one hand and diviners or witchdoctors on the other hand. The former mainly provide herbs to their clients, the latter are said to make use of supernatural powers in their healing practices. These supernatural powers help them to cure and to get to know the cause of the health-problems, which will most times be considered to be witchcraft. Frequently a witchdoctor will identify someone in the patient's social environment as a witch and offer his patient to take revenge on this person.

Herbalists and witchdoctors cannot always strictly be distinguished. Some Malawians allege that they often don't know whether there are supernatural powers involved or not. Herbalists use traditional medicines also for 'supernatural' health-problems, like those caused by witchcraft or by violation of certain taboos. Witchdoctors or diviners do not only use supernatural powers but also herbal medicines. As many Malawians do not want to get involved in witchcraft, witchdoctors will often be requested to restrict themselves to curing, instead of pointing out who has been bewitching or taking revenge on this person.

Especially poor Malawians and those living in villages will consult traditional healers. Traditional healers are in general less expensive than western medical care and hospitals are often located too far away from the villages. Certain health-problems, like sexually transmitted diseases and infertility are considered especially curable by traditional healers. When western medical care does not help, Malawians will resort to traditional healing. In addition, when people think witchcraft is at work they either prefer a witchdoctor above the hospital or combine western medical-care with traditional healing methods. Witchcraft suspicions are likely to arise if the disease is considered extreme and strange, because of awkward symptoms, unexpected onset or long duration. Also when Malawians become ill while having arguments with others in their environment, or when they expect others to envy them, people will tend to attribute their illness to witchcraft.

Birth rituals

In Malawi, pregnancy and birth are surrounded many few beliefs, taboos and rituals. For example, in order to protect the life of the baby men are not allowed to have intercourse with other women during pregnancy and women should not put salt in relish or eggs. Birth rituals can be divided into two groups; those aimed at protection of the baby against physical, natural problems and those aimed at protection against supernatural forces, like witchcraft. Babies are considered especially vulnerable for witchcraft as witches are said to like eating foetuses and babies. Common customs around birth are to bath the baby in water with traditional medicines, or to give the baby a necklace, which frequently contains medicines as well. Both customs are said to make the fontanel grow tight or to protect against witchcraft. Note that they thus have a dual function; protection against both natural and supernatural problems. Frequently it will not be clear which of these two functions a birth ritual is expected to fulfill.

Traditional funerals

Different kinds of traditional funerals can be distinguished. There is the institutionalized form, like funerals for deceased chiefs or Nyau-members (see above). Nyau-funerals for example, are clearly distinguishable from a Christian- or Muslim-funeral. During this funeral the masked figures show up. Excesses of violence are said to occur at these happenings, and people sometimes get injured. Less institutionalized –and less notorious- 'traditional funerals' are those, which can be typed as 'Christian', or 'Muslim' but contain different traditional religious elements. Examples of such traditional elements are the shaving of hair or washing of the hands of people who attended the funeral. Both customs are said to prevent the spirits of the dead to stick with the people after the funeral. Another explanation for the washing of the hands is that people have to get rid of the sand of the grave, as otherwise witches might get the sand into their possession and use this for evil purposes. Another known traditional custom is that after the funeral people go back to the graveyard, to check whether they can see animal-traces, for example of a hyena. If these signs are found it is said that the deceased turned into the animal, which means that he or she has used traditional medicines or even that he or she was a witch

Rain-rituals

a. Praying to ancestral spirits

Rain is of vital need in hot and poor countries like Malawi. Traditionally ancestral spirits are considered to be the providers of rain in Malawi. In yearly rain-calling rituals people pray to the ancestors to send rain and make small offerings like food and beer. There is some disagreement about whether people still pray to ancestral spirits for rain or whether this has been replaced by praying to the Christian God. Nevertheless, it seems that especially in the rural areas, people do still pray to ancestral spirits as well.

b. Rain-withholding

Many Malawians assert there are people who can prevent the rains from falling by using witchcraft. This is reported as well on radio, television and in newspapers. Thus when the rain season does not start in time there are Malawians –especially in the villages- who accuse people of withholding the rains. Mostly the accused are elderly women or men, who are in general 'prime suspects' of witchcraft. The actions taken against the suspects will differ somewhat per ethnic group and village, but it will certainly not be pleasant for the suspects.

4.2 Prevalence of ATR in Malawi

The ethnographic description shows what kind of ATR-practices and believes are relevant for contemporary Malawians. But for whom is this ATR exactly relevant? Is ATR in Malawi at the end of the twentieth century not becoming a historical relic, in which these days only the elderly, the uneducated, the conservatives and those living far away 'in the bush' are involved? Is ATR restricted to certain ethnic groups?

The relation between some demographic factors and ATR-involvement will be discussed here, because it will give an idea to which extent and for which strata of the Malawian population ATR is alive. Normally discourse analytic research does not deal with 'fixed givens' –factors like age or ethnicity- until their local procedural relevance can be demonstrated (Ten Have, 1999d; Antaki and Widdicombe, 1998). Demographic factors are only taken into account when conversation partners can be observed to use, or to orient themselves to, these factors as resource in their accounting-practices (Antaki & Widdicombe, 1998). Later on in this thesis I will show how Malawian Christians do indeed orient to and use certain demographic factors in their accounting-practices.

Overall, all ethnic groups in Malawi are to some extent involved in ATR and all ethnic-groups deal with more or less the same ATR-practices and beliefs. Certain ATR-practices and -beliefs are especially associated with certain ethnic-groups. For example, initiations are especially associated with the Yao and Chewa, whereby the Yao initiation-ceremonies are notorious amongst others due to their practice of circumcision, the Chewa initiations because of their violent character.

It seems likely that ATR-practices and beliefs will be more prevalent among people who have had less education. At school Malawians are exposed to alternative, western scientific worldviews (Wendroff, 1989), which increases chances that the irrefutable 'truth' of ATR is reconsidered. In addition schools in Malawi frequently have strong connections with Christianity as many were founded by missionaries and are often based at mission-places. ATR will not exactly be promoted at these mission-schools. However, even if ATR is more prevalent among the lower educated, this does not mean that ATR is restricted to a small minority: most Malawians are only moderately educated. About 30 percent of the Malawian population has never attended school, 60 percent only attended primary school (National Statistical Office, 1998). Of the population above five years 58 percent is literate (National Statistical Office, 1998). In addition, although in general education might decrease ATR-involvement, during fieldwork it became clear that ATR is certainly not *ir*relevant to educated Malawians.

ATR will in general be more 'alive' in rural than urban areas. On average poverty is higher, and education-level lower in rural areas. Therefore village-people will in general be confronted less with alternative western 'world-views' and alternatives for ATR-practices and beliefs, via for example television, books or trade-relations. However, urbanization in Malawi is very low; only 14 percent of the population lives in urban areas. Thus when practices are said to be restricted to the villages, this means that a large part of the population will be familiar with them. Secondly, when Malawians live in town, they maintain strong links with their home-villages where part of their family will still be living. People periodically return to their home-villages, for example in case of initiation or death. One only needs to realize the height of death rates and low life expectancy in Malawi (see appendix C) to imagine that return to the home-village is not a rare event.

Also elderly can be expected to be more involved in ATR. On average more elderly will live in villages and they will have received less then average education. The parents of the older Malawians lived when no one had ever heard of the white-men and their Christianity. However, ATR appears not to be restricted to the elderly. Participate observation in the first year course taught at the University of Malawi made clear that students were able to tell about ATR-practices and beliefs they encountered in their own lives. Also the research-essays, which students wrote during this course, revealed that young Malawians are acquainted with many ATR-practices and beliefs. In addition, the three young Malawians between 16 and 19 years of age who were interviewed did not show to have less knowledge about and experience with ATR then older respondents, as table 2 shows (appendix B).

Thus, many traditional practices and especially beliefs are relevant for all kinds of people, regardless of ethnicity, educational or social-economic background, place of living and age, a fact also clearly shown in Malawian newspapers.

4.3 Christianity in Malawi

In the preceding paragraphs, African Traditional Religion and its prevalence among different strata of the Malawian population have been described. As this study's research-topic is Malawians' dual religious involvement in ATR and Christianity, in this paragraph the relevance of Christianity in the lives of Malawians will be sketched. It should be born in mind that this is just a general sketch, as this research did not focus on the reconstruction of Christianity in contemporary Malawi.

Various sources (National Statistical Office, 1998; Landenwijzer Bijeen, 1996) differ somewhat with regard to estimated numbers of Christians and other religions in Malawi. On average, 70% of the population is estimated to be Christian and 20% to be Muslim, leaving 10% for non-religious people and 'traditionalists'. The Christian population in Malawi may contain 40% Protestant CCAP, 25% Roman Catholics and 5% Anglicans.

When one spends some time in Malawi it immediately becomes clear how central Christianity is in daily life in Malawi[3]. There are numerous church-buildings, some very small and simple, some large and built in a

---

[3] The same can be said about the Islam, but this religion is not the focus of this research

typical European style. Many Malawian cars have stickers on their windows with texts like 'I love Jesus'. People want to know to which church you belong, and thus know each other's religious affiliation. Often Malawians wear, clearly visible, necklaces with a cross. On Sunday, groups of people gather to attend church, neatly dressed and with their bibles under their arms. Members of the same church clearly form a social group together. For example, when one member of the church dies the other members are informed as quickly as possible and called upon to gather for the funeral. In conversations people frequently refer to God, in general depicting Him as an almighty God who can help people in their lives. Common expressions are 'with God's help', 'if God wants', 'God bless you'. Regularly shopkeepers have painted Chichewa names on their shops, which refer to God and Christianity like 'Mulungu apatsa', which means 'God gives'. It should be mentioned however that some names refer to ancestors and witchcraft as well. People state that in times of drought they pray to God, hoping that God will bring rain. Sickness and death are other moments in life in which Christianity appears to be important for Malawians. Malawians stress the importance of receiving a decent Christian funeral when they die. People say to pray to God to get healed and there are quite a few Christian healers in Malawi; people who claim to be able to heal people due to a Godly gift.

Thus, Christianity appears to be quite central in the lives of Malawians. Indeed like Schoffeleers (1983) said, the missionaries and scholars who claimed that Africans were Christian at Sunday and heathen during the week, appear wrong.

4.4 Policy of the church: Official decrees and respondents' assertions

When accounting for ATR and dual religious involvement, it can be expected that Christian Malawians will orient to the decrees of the churches of which they are members. In this paragraph the official policy of the CCAP and Roman-Catholic-Church in Malawi concerning dual involvement in Christianity and ATR will be discussed. Hereby some historical context of the church-policy will be provided as well. It should be mentioned that this research did not aim at a reconstruction of the church-policy with regard to ATR. Although respondents have been asked about the church-policy, the aim of this study was not to find out the 'truth' about church policies. For this study it is more important to see how respondents depict the policy to the western researcher and how they use these descriptions in their accounts, something which will be investigated when the Malawian Christians' accounting-practices are discussed into detail.

When the missionaries arrived in Malawi around 1870[4] (de Jong, 1994), they zealously started to convert the Malawian population. Both the Protestant Central Church of African Presbyterian[5] and Roman-Catholics put much effort in making the local population forsake their own indigenous religion, something which 'conversion' seems to demand by definition. ATR was denounced as backward, primitive and pagan (Chingota, 1995; Tengatenga, 1998). In later years both churches took up a more lenient stance with regard to ATR. Missionaries emphasised that ATR contained both bad and good aspects, and the latter should be used as a starting-point to work up to the 'true' faith of Christianity (Chingota, 1995; Chakanza, 1998).

Since the Second Vatican Council in 1965 the Roman-Catholic church has officially adopted a policy of 'inculturation' (Chakanza, 1998). In contrast to the early missionaries who professed to bring the one and only true belief to the people, the Vatican II declared that each culture can and should have it's own true Christianity. The CCAP adopted a policy, which is similar to the Catholics' 'inculturation', which they called 'contextualisation' (Chakanza, personal communication, December 1999). In general, the CCAP seems to be more careful and hesitant in introducing ATR in church. She restricts herself to tolerate the practices, which Malawians stubbornly keep performing, whereas certain progressive Roman-Catholic clergy not only accept persistent practices but also even try to revive ATR (Chakanza, personal communication, December 1999). Roman Catholicism seems to leave more room for ATR as in this denomination bible-texts are interpreted less strictly than within the CCAP. In addition, Catholicism has congruencies with ATR in the centrality of rituals and belief in ancestral spirits or Catholic saints (*op cit.*).

Thus, in theory one would expect that CCAP members condemn ATR and dual religious involvement more than members of the Roman Catholic Church do. However, in practice it seems that the ways in which CCAP and Roman Catholics –both clergy and laity -deal with ATR hardly differ. To begin with, both Catholic's and CCAP' awareness of the churches' attempts to 'inculturate or 'contextualise' can be questioned: many interviewed

---

[4] See appendix C for exact years of arrival in Malawi of different Christian denominations

[5] In 1924 the Free Church of Scotland, the Church of Scotland and Dutch Reformed Church were merged into this Central Church of Africa Presbyterian

parishioners and even clergy appeared to have only vague ideas about the meaning of the inculturation-policy or the contextualisation of the CCAP.

In addition, until now both 'inculturation' and 'contextualisation' most times do not go further than a rather shallow fusion of Christianity with traditional symbols, like traditional instruments or traditional dress. In the Catholic Church, a few clergy do go further, for example by combining traditional and Christian rites (Bishop Kalilombe, personal communication, December 1999). But these progressive clergy are a – controversial - exception. Neither the cry for inculturation of the Vatican, nor the contextualisation-policy of the CCAP, seems to have led to an embracing of ATR within Christianity by local clergy or laity in Malawi. In the interviews, Roman Catholics did not report a more lenient stance of their church concerning ATR then CCAP did about their own church. It seems that until today, the performing of certain ATR-practices is not encouraged, but rather condemned or even punished by the church. Respondents reported that Christians, who deal with ATR can be brought before the church-council, could be temporarily excluded from receiving the sacraments, or even – temporarily- excommunicated.

Nor did Roman Catholic respondents profess to be more involved in ATR or to have themselves a more positive opinion about introducing ATR in the church. When examples of inculturation were discussed in the interviews, the majority of the respondents -both Catholics and CCAP, both laity and clergy- either did not see the need for this inculturation or, more frequently, even straightforwardly rejected it. Indeed, it seems that implementation of inculturation-policy often does not have the results it was meant to have. For example, both the CCAP and the Roman Catholic Church designed their own intitiation ceremony to offer a Christian alternative for the traditional initiations. The churches' purpose was that Malawians would finally stop this -already forbidden- traditional practice. Nevertheless, Malawians have continued to send their children to 'chinamwali', possibly in combination with attendance of Christian initiation (Chakanza, 1998). Apparently many Malawians did not and do not perceive Christian-rites as an appealing alternative to 'chinamwali'.

On the other hand, both CCAP and Roman-Catholic-respondents reported that the churches in Malawi do tolerate certain ATR-practices and beliefs. It is said that churches sometimes ignore the performing of some ATR-practices, like traditional funerals. In other instances, Malawians are only asked to temporarily refrain from ATR, namely while engaged in

Christianity. For example mothers who come to church are asked to take off the necklaces of their babies, *while in church*. People reporting problems to their clergy related to witchcraft are told to go and seek help *outside* the church. It seems that Malawian Christians' involvement in ATR outside the church is often not commented on. It might be the best and only option for churches to claim to reject ATR but to ignore the practising of it. For, although the churches have been condemning and discouraging ATR-involvement, Malawian Christians persistently hang on to their indigenous religious tradition. Or might there be alternative explanations for this ambivalent stance of the church and its clergy? This question can be answered when more insight is gained into the way in which Christian Malawians, orient in talk to Christian's involvement in ATR.

4.5 ATR among respondents: claims about involvement

In has been argued that many Malawians are involved in both Christianity and ATR. As this research deals with accounting-practices of concrete individuals it is worthwhile to see to what extent the interviewed Christian Malawians professed to be involved in ATR.

Table 2 in appendix B gives a first impression of the interviewed Christian Malawians' involvement in ATR-practices and –beliefs, as asserted in the interviews. The table shows that quite a few respondents claim to perform, or to have performed several ATR-practices and to have certain 'beliefs'. All respondents are involved to some extend in ATR, though some more than others are. Note that table 2 suggests that witchcraft is an omnipresent reality in Malawi: it is the only ATR-aspect, which is considered to be 'real' by, and is thus relevant in the lives of, all 14 respondents.

It should be mentioned that if respondents claim that ATR-practices and beliefs are not relevant in their lives, this does not automatically imply that they are not familiar with them. For example, although Mrs. T claims to be hardly involved in ATR, in the interview she does give examples of ATR-practices and -beliefs she encountered in her life. In addition, if Malawians don't practice ATR or do not belief in it, this does not necessarily mean that they condemn ATR. For instance, in general Mrs. T respects the individual points of view of people who do want to perform certain ATR-practices or have certain beliefs.

What is important to note is that, as can be seen in Table 3, it is often not possible to categorize respondents according to a dichotomy of 'practising' versus 'not practising', 'believing' versus 'not believing'. Many respondents express doubt in relation to ATR-aspects. They profess not to know whether they will perform a practice in the future, or they claim not to know whether the belief is true or not. As table 2 shows, expressions of doubt co-occur with both acknowledgements and denials of ATR-practices and beliefs. This means that respondents can at the same time admit they will perform a practice and doubt they will do this. Or, they both doubt that a 'belief' like witchcraft is real and admit its reality. Furthermore, with regard to ATR-beliefs it appeared to be necessary to distinguish between assertions about 'belief in' and 'reality of' ATR-aspects. Respondents can claim the reality of an ATR-'belief' –for example by asserting that ancestral spirits and witches are *real*- but at the same time that they *don't believe* in it. Later on we will return to these issues, which make it difficult to straightforwardly determine to what extent respondents are involved in ATR, and to what extent ATR is relevant for him or her.

Conclusion

In the ethnographic description several ATR-practices and –beliefs, which are relevant in Malawi nowadays, were discussed. In the discussion of the prevalence of ATR it became clear that ATR is to a large extend alive for different people from different strata of the population. At the same time, observation of daily life shows that Christianity is central in Malawi. Although Malawians and other African people are frequently said to turn to ATR at so called 'crisis-moments' in life, like death and sickness (Meyer, 1994; Chakanza, personal communication, November 1999), Malawians appear to turn to Christianity as well at these moments. Apparently ATR and Christianity coexist in the lives of many Malawians. It has been said that the Malawian churches have become more lenient with regard to ATR and that especially the Roman Catholic Church tries to bring ATR and Christianity together. Nevertheless, the interviewed Malawian Christians who were interviewed for this study pointed out that in practice –whether protestant or catholic- clergy frequently still disapprove of dual religious involvement. One becomes curious how the Malawian Christians who belong to a church that in general disapproves of ATR-involvement, but perform certain ATR practices or have certain ATR beliefs, account for this 'dual involvement'. Therefore, in the next chapter accounting-practices in concrete patches of conversation will be investigated.

5. Accounting Malawian Christians

If churches in Malawi are opposed to several ATR practices and beliefs of their members, Malawian Christians in Malawi dealing with ATR seems to have something to account for. What do Christian Malawians themselves have to say about this issue? What do they assert when a white researcher asks them both about their ATR-involvement and about the church-policy?

The next paragraphs will deal with the first research question: what kind of accounts do Christian Malawians give for involvement in ATR.

5.1 Problematising ATR: Identity-talk

The interviewed Christian Malawians frequently subscribe to the rejecting stance of the church, both when they are directly asked to reflect on the church-policy and when the church-policy was not mentioned before. As all respondents are or have been to some extent involved in ATR-practices or -beliefs themselves (see table 2, appendix B), it is interesting to investigate how Christian Malawians exactly reject ATR in conversation. In this paragraph the use of some accounts which respondents use to problematise Christians' ATR –involvement will be examined.

Legislative Rejection

Subsequent extracts will show how, and with which results, respondents exactly orient in their talk to the rejecting stance of the church.

Extract 1 R2 2/16[6]

(Interviewer asks whether respondent knows about practices the church disapproves of)
1. R Practices oh yes, like if someone who is a Christian has died he is not allowed to there

---

[6] 'R2' means respondent 2. '2/6' is based on the division of interview data into documents and segments which the computer-program Kwalitan, which was used for analysis, requires. The interviews have been divided over 4 documents (6,7,8 and 9) because each document can contain a limited amount of interview data. Each interview has been divided into segments, in general containing one main question with some probing sub-questions. Thus 2/6 means document 2, segment 6.

2	became a traditional healer who can be on the funeral, saying that oh I want to go to the graveyard so
3	that the witchcraft can not go there. That cannot be allowed by the leaders of the church. Because
4	these two things can not go together it is not allowed to a Christian or even to have something
5	the graveyard which is never (..?) the traditional healer, yeah.
6.	I These two things can't go together, which two things can't go together?
7.	R I mean the traditional medicine and the Christianity, yeah.

Extract 2. R12 9/5

1.	I Hmhm, I don't know did you go to an initiation-rite yourself?
2.	R No. I didn't go.
3.	I Why not?
4.	R All right, I was waiting for that question, hahaha
5.	I Hahaha, yeah okay, go ahead
6.	R Well, just because of religious belief or Christianity. You know the Roman-Catholics, in the past, they
7.	did not believe in initiations at all. Anybody who was initiated was taken as an outcast in the Roman-
8.	Catholic. Because ehm, initiation-programs were connected with witchcraft and the like. So this was
9.	greatly prohibited, it was not allowed in the Catholics. So it was a rule that was agreed by the Catholics
10.	that nobody should go for initiations.

(Respondent explains hereafter that the Roman Catholic Church still forbids initiations, but that the difference is that they offer their own Christian initiation these days)

Extract 3. R4 4/12

1	I But what do you think about it when Malawians try to ask their ancestral spirits for protection?
2	R Eh it means that they are now mixing Christianity with ATR. Because in the ATR it's where we
3	believe that eh our ancestral spirits could protect us, could speak to God for anything, could and again

4   God would have speaked to us through the eh spirits. So when we still do that then it means we have
5   not changed. We have not changed, we have not really been converted to Christianity. So this we
6   don't like and we must change. So that now we really show that we are devoted Christians and not
7   mixing the two, no.
8   I You don't think that people can believe at the same time in for example ancestral spirits and in the
9   Christian God or
10 R   Yes, that is taking place, that is taking place. But it's very dangerous. Because it's now like having
11 two masters, haha. One can not serve two masters. So, that's the danger. We ought to leave the other
12 master and then follow and then we'll be (...?) one master and he must be Jesus Christ. So this is what
13 Jesus Christ initiated the church and he left the church in our hands so that we use it and we'll be in the church and then he finds us there in the church.

In extract 1, the respondent rejects Christians' use of traditional medicine (line 8) and having a traditional healer at a funeral. The respondent in extract 2 says that he did not go to initiation 'just because of Christianity' (line 6). In extract 3 the respondent problematises Christians' praying to ancestral spirits. All three respondents give a similar type of account when rejecting ATR-practices, which can be labelled as 'Legislative Rejection'. Four features can be identified as characteristic for the 'Legislative Rejection' account. First, respondents rejecting ATR by means of this account make relevant the church and its laws. In so doing, the church is depicted as an external body with an authority to tell its members what to do or what not to do. This is a way in which respondents can strengthen their rejection of ATR as they show that their rejection is not contingent and idiosyncratic. The Church forbids dual involvement, and this is an inevitable, general law, which true Christians are to abide.

Second, respondents who use 'Legislative Rejection' frequently and repetitively use imperative and prohibitive phrases like ' they must', 'they ought' 'not supposed', and 'not allowed'. Hereby they underline the strict, irrefutable character of the rejection, which is often sustained by a resolute, accentuated intonation. See for example the short, stressed denial of respondent 12 in extract ' No.' Followed by the very short elaboration: 'I didn't go.' (line 2). The abrupt ending of this answer is remarkable, among others because respondent 12 is quite eloquent. In line 6 it becomes clear that the respondent's answer is certainly not this short because he is not able or not willing to give a more elaborate explanation. By his assertion 'Alright, I was waiting for that question, hahaha' and by his extensive elucidation (lines 6-10), he suggests to be quite eager to explain why he did not attend initiation. By telling about the church history he puts himself forward as knowledgeable about his church and makes Christianity relevant for his life and for his way of acting. By saying *'well, just* because of Christianity' he puts effort in constructing the ecclesiastical authority as taken for granted. Thus, the respondent positions himself in this extract as a devoted Christian who therefore, self-evidentially, did not attend initiation-ceremonies. It should be mentioned that at another moment in the interview this respondent makes clear that he did not wholeheartedly reject initiation. He tells that when he was young he did not like it that he was not initiated, as he was laughed at by his non-Christian initiated friends.

Third, in Legislative Rejection-accounts the use of maxims can be observed. In extract 3, respondent 4 makes clear that conversion to Christianity requires change, requires leaving behind ATR. In line 6 he says that one

> **Box. 2** Concepts like 'identity-positions', 'identity-talk' and 'positioning' will regularly reoccur in this thesis. It is important to realize that they do not refer to a 'real' identity in an essentialistic sense, which is hidden in people or which people have, and which makes them do, think and say things. Identity-related concepts, which are used in this thesis, are rather considered to refer to identity- categories, which people can be ascribed or circumvent to be ascribed and ascribe to others. Identity- categories are of relevance in this study as far as they are made relevant in talk and are consequential for interactions (see Antaki & Widdicombe, 1999).

should not mix the two, for, 'one can not serve two masters.' In extract 1 the respondent used another very common expression: 'the two can not go together' (line 4). By using this kind of maxims, respondents invite their conversation-partner to accept a statement –in this case the strict incompatibility of ATR and Christianity - as an irrefutable, commonsensical 'fact'. It's a convincing-technique, making further explication redundant and forestalling critical questions.

A fourth feature of the Legislative Rejection account is related to the use of general statements or maxims: respondents using this account regularly speak in plural and general terms. It is noticeable for example that in extract 3 the respondent uses himself the abstract term 'ATR'. In extract 1 the respondent's phrasing *the* traditional medicine and the Christianity (line 8), in extract 2 the respondent speaks about *the* Catholics. In addition, this respondent refers to 'anybody' who would become an outcast after initiation, and 'nobody' who should be initiated. Using such general terms sustains the construction of rejection of ATR as something, which is generally valid and accepted. In addition, it contributes to the creation of the mutually exclusive, reified categories of ATR versus Christianity. Although they might speak about specific practices or beliefs which can not go together with Christianity, 'Legislative Rejection' strikes as a declaration of incompatibility of two monolithic religions: 'Christianity' versus 'ATR'.

By putting forward this account respondents make clear that Christians should not deal with ATR or certain ATR-aspects, *because they are Christians*. Thus, 'Legislative Rejection' is an unconditional type of rejection for Christians; once you are a Christian ATR-practices and beliefs -and often ATR in general- is 'out'. Especially clergy put forward 'Legislative Rejection', although the laity uses this type of accounting as well.

Especially extract 3 demonstrates that Christian Malawians, using Legislative Rejection can not only construct contrasting categories of two religions but also contrasting categories of people; 'devoted Christians' versus 'those involved in ATR' or 'those not converted' or 'pagans'. In talk like it occurs in extracts 1, 2 and 3, respondents position themselves as people who are knowledgeable about the incompatibility of ATR and Christianity and who adhere to the commandments of the church. Hereby respondents implicitly contrast themselves with others who don't abide by church rules because they are 'mixing the two'. Thus, by using 'Legislative Rejection' respondents can position themselves as devoted Christians.

Christian Moralizing

The foregoing might raise the question whether Malawian Christians merely follow church-rules and only reject ATR because the church tells them so. The next extracts will shed some light on this.

Extract 4 R10 3/24

1. I   Jaja so is it that you think if they believe traditional healers can cure them then they should go if they want to
2. R   If they believe that they can go. But if maybe they just go there just because like, their parents told
3. them to, or like there are even people from town actually go there maybe just to get rich. They want
4. maybe the (reduction) of the what witchdoctor tell them ah (kill?) your husband and children.
5. Something like that. Maybe just to be a witch. So I don't, I don't know. I don't know. I feel like the
6. witchdoctor. Actually I can feel like it's like, something like evil. I don't know. It's not right. I don't know.
7. I   And it's not right, in what sense?
8. R   That maybe like when you go to the hospital, you don't actually, maybe you are ill, they heal you.
9. Maybe like you go there, they start lying to you like maybe they say it's your sister who bewitched
10. you. Actually have hatred towards your sister. And then that's real bad. I don't know, it's real bad to
11. make you hurt somebody who is actually innocent.
12. I   Hm, okay. And do you think that there's for example, that Christians shouldn't go to traditional
13. healers or doesn't that matter?
14. R   I think you shouldn't go. Because I don't know, its like ah he will make you, what they do actually
15. what they do, *what* I have heard it's like he'll make you hate somebody who you are not suppose to
16. hate and that's real bad. Like you do some things which you're not supposed to do.(…)
17. I   Jaja. But ehm, can you explain maybe some more why is it then not good for a Christian to go there?
18. R   It's not good because it's like. Jeeh.
19. I   Haha.
20. R   That question (.) hm. it's like, I don't know, but I feel like it's not good.

21. I   Hmhm, you just think Christians shouldn't do that because it's not (.)
22. R   Yeah because it's like they can pray; God can help them. Why should they go there. There's no need
23.   for them to go there, actually they have got God?) .(They belief in them?)(...?)
24. I   Hmhm
25. R   So I don't think it's alright.

In line 3 of extract 4 the respondent states that people can go to the traditional healer. However, in the very same line she also starts to problematise the consulting of traditional healers. In line 7 she clearly rejects use of witchdoctors. Repetitive use of strong negative adjectives like 'real bad' 'evil', by a stressing intonation (line 10) and by saying 'I feel' (line 6), the respondent makes available the inference that it is not a factual statement but a moral judgement of which she is personally convinced.

The account, which the respondent uses here to problematise ATR, can be called 'Christian Moralizing'. Repetitively attributing negative adjectives to ATR-practices or –beliefs, especially 'bad' or 'not good', while using a stressing intonation, are characteristics of 'Christian moralizing'. Respondents reject different ATR-aspects by using this account. For example they reject Nyau-practices because they harm or even kill people, or disapprove of initiation because girls are sometimes more or less raped. In relation to witchcraft and witchdoctors, respondents frequently say to disapprove the falsely accusing people of witchcraft. Although it's not a principled necessity to be a Christian to condemn these practices, respondents frequently attend to Christianity, the bible or God when using this moralizing account. See how in line 23 the respondent accounts for her statement that Christians shouldn't go to traditional healers by making relevant their ability to pray and seek help from God.

Respondents regularly make clear that Malawian Christians, who perform practices or have beliefs, which they condemn, on moral grounds, are less devoted Christians. However, it should be mentioned that they do this predominantly when the interviewer asks what the consequences of ATR-involvement are for someone's Christian faith.

By engaging in 'Christian Moralizing', respondents can construct 'virtuous' Christianity as superior to 'vile' ATR. Also in other accounts respondents can construct Christianity as superior, emphasizing the importance and value of Christianity. For example, a common way to construct Christianity as superior to ATR is by predicting that ATR or 'tradition' is fading away and will inevitably die out, because Christianity will replace it. Respondents portray the extinction of ATR and replacement by Christianity as not only inevitable and unproblematic, but even fortunate. By upgrading Christianity and downgrading ATR and thus constructing Christianity as superior, respondents can position themselves as Christians who are committed to Christianity and not to ATR. Thus, the rejecting of ATR-practices or beliefs as immoral, in contrast to Christian practices and beliefs, as can be observed in extract 4, is a way to position oneself as devoted Christian.

Conclusion

In this section we have seen respondents subscribing to the point of view of the church, which in general condemns ATR-involvement. Different types of accounts have been observed which problematise ATR. These accounts are in different ways related to Christianity. Respondents can construct ATR and Christianity as mutually exclusive entities, or at least as contrasting categories. Regularly Malawian Christians make clear that Christianity is more worthy than ATR. They do this by showing to agree with the laws of the church which reject ATR, or by condemning ATR as 'bad' or 'evil', and at the same time contrasting bad ATR with Christianity which is more virtuous or in other ways superior to ATR.

Because respondents make relevant Christianity and being Christian, the problematising accounts discussed so far are unconditional. The respondents can make clear by using Legislative Rejection or Christian Moralizing that once people are Christians, in principle one should not be involved in ATR-practices or beliefs. ATR should not be an option anymore. The sincerity of faith of those Malawian Christians who are involved in ATR is at stake. By making relevant Christianity and its rules and morals, respondents not only show to reject ATR but they also position themselves as good, devoted Christians. Thus, respondents giving a legislative rejection account can be said to engage in 'identity talk' (cf. Slugoski and Ginsburg, 1989) (see box 2).

Intermezzo I: The questions left unanswered

So far, we have seen that Malawian Christians orient to ATR and dual involvement in ATR and Christianity in a way, which reflects the rejecting stance of the church. Malawian Christians position themselves in a way, which must have been the early missionaries' ideal. Yet, it has been argued that the mission did not achieve a complete success of erasure of ATR, neither in Malawi nor in other African countries (Meyer, 1994; Warkentin, 1996). Also table 3 shows that the respondents, also those who appear until now to reject ATR, did profess ATR-involvement as well. It might be that Christianity and ATR 'can not go together'. But apparently those who make this claim can still assert to be involved in at least some ATR-practices and beliefs. Look for example at the following extract which will give some food for thought.

EXTRACT R2 2/2
1 I   But do you also think then that Malawians who are also Christians, that they shouldn't go to
2 traditional healers actually?
3 R   I think that is better, because when most of the Malawians can go to the traditional healer I think that
4 will make them not to believe in God. Yes.
5 I   Ja Ja But it doesn't, it can't go together, that you for example that you <u>and</u> go to the traditional healer
6 <u>and</u> that you believe in God?
7 R   Ah no, it can't go together.
8 I   And, but, because I am wondering because I think you told me yesterday that you consulted some
9 traditional healers sometimes.
10 R   Yes
11 I   Ehm but you are also Christian...
12 R   Yah.
13.I   How do you, haha, see that then?
14.R   Oh, on my part I do this because ah I do believe God. Not that I believe on his traditional healers, yah
15.only what I do is that, I do it because of some what, something which might happen at home is what
16.made me to go to the traditional healers. But not that I believe of them, yes.

This extract strikes as ambiguous and contradictory. The respondent declares consulting traditional healers and believing in God as incompatible (lines 3,4 and 7), at the same time he declares to have consulted traditional healers himself. Among the interview-data are many more of such extracts, which strike, from a western perspective, as 'illogical'. In order to come to an understanding of these ambivalent research-findings, further examination of accounting-practices is necessary.

5. 2 Problematising ATR: Pragmatic-talk

The reasons which are put forward to reject ATR are not always directly related to Christianity, and thus accounts anti-ATR which Christian Malawians give are not always unconditional. In this paragraph, some problematising accounts will be discussed in which respondents do not –at least not directly- make relevant Christianity.

Debunking

As becomes clear from the ethnographic description in chapter 4, many ATR-beliefs and especially ATR–practices are often attributed certain societal functions. However, one way in which respondents appear to problematise ATR is by suggesting that ATR-practices don't have a function at all. They frequently reject ATR-aspects because they are useless or primitive. For example, initiation rites are commonly said to have the societal function of contributing to the becoming of worthy, knowledgeable adults in Malawian society. However, many respondents debunk initiation by emphasizing that children are taught things they should not (yet) know, like sex, and by pointing out that the things which are said to be taught at initiations can be learnt just as well, and probably better, at school or from family members. In this way of accounting, which can be called 'Debunking', respondents construct ATR as trivial and irrelevant. Especially if ATR- practices are *meant* to be useful -like in case of traditional healing or initiation ceremonies- 'Debunking' is a clear rejection.

Malawian Christians use 'Debunking' not only when talking about practices: this type of account can also pertain to certain traditional beliefs, as can be observed in the next extract.

Extract 7 R 79/8

1   I   But ehm do you think it's possible that someone ehm, so if people tell the story then they tell about
2   someone who uses witchcraft in a way or something to prevent the rain from falling. Ehm, is that
3   possible?

4 R It is not possible. I don't believe it. ... It's not true
5 I No it isn't?
6 R (laughs loudly) There are so many reasons why rains come and why rains don't come. Scientifically
7 that doesn't work
8 you can't associate passing of an axe with a fire with the coming of rain (refers to ritual described
9 before)
10 I Hmhm, ja
11 R (laughs)
(respondent explains why God can influence scientifically the weather)
12 R what is in a bamboo and what is in the axe and the combination of heat of the fire to the axe, hahaha
13 I And you don't think for example, I don't' know that that combination then of the bamboo and the heat
14 that that evokes a kind of magic power, which also like a kind of God changes scientifically the winds
15 and all that whereby the rain comes?
16 R I don't think so. They work on coincidence. I don't know sometimes maybe they'll relate it to God.
17 Our God may not work in a favourable way. It is a coincidence that will make people be believers on
18 something which is just done on a trial basis or because they have heard or somebody told them.

Respondent 7 debunks a rain calling-ritual by asserting that doing something with bamboo, an axe and making fire can not influence the coming of rain (line 7, 8, 9). In line 9 he stresses his disbelief in the working of the ritual by using three similar phrases in a row: 'It is not possible. I don't believe it. ... It's not true.' (line 4). He does not make this statement in a neutral way; he ridiculises the practice and belief by laughing much and loudly (lines 6, 11 and 14). This aids the respondent's construction of himself as a disbeliever.

The respondent in extract 7 makes clear that he rejects the 'belief' in rain calling-rituals because of his scientific knowledge (line 6). Referring to scientific knowledge is one of the ways in which respondents debunk ATR, the other one being reporting one's education or European experiences when debunking ATR-aspects. Such reports are not only a way to debunk ATR, but also to position oneself as belonging to modern and western people. By making relevant western knowledge or experiences respondents can put themselves forward as people who differ from the 'plain folk' in Malawi who 'ignorantly' believe in and practice ATR aspects. Again it appears that Malawian Christians can engage in 'identity talk' when problematising ATR. Not only Christian identities can be constructed but also the identity of the modern, educated Malawian.

Sometimes debunking respondents refer to Christianity in their problematising accounts. Besides coincidence and natural processes, God is sometimes put forward as alternative explanation for the working of ATR-practices. For example, one respondent stated that if rain did fall after a rain calling-ritual this probably would have been the work of God to whom so many people were praying for rain as well. Thus, Malawian Christian respondents can simultaneously reject ATR for rather pragmatic reasons –it does not work-, position themselves as modern Malawians and as devoted Christian who don't serve 'two masters'. Hence, the Malawian Christians who put forward 'Debunking' both engage in what can be called 'practical talk' and 'identity talk'.

Note that this discursive strategy of 'Debunking' shows that Malawian Christians don't have to reject ATR unconditionally. Respondents using this account don't construct ATR and Christianity as mutual exclusive. For, why wouldn't Christian Malawians perform certain practices or have certain beliefs if they are not considered being clearly nonsensical?

Pointing out Risk

Sometimes respondents use stronger 'artillery' to debunk ATR-aspects than showing that performing of certain ATR-practices or having certain ATR-'beliefs' is silly and ridiculous. See what the respondent in the next extract has to say about traditional healers.

Extract 8 .R3 1-25

1 I   So is it then that normally if you are sick you go to the doctor, and maybe if it doesn't work then you
2 consider going to the traditional healer, but then you also should have an idea that there might be
3 someone in your environment who might want to harm you, or...Is that what you mean?
4 R   Yeah I don't suspect anyone to harm me, and the second thing I don't

believe in traditional healers
5 because they don't have measurements of giving medicine to people;
6 I Measurements...
7 R They can just give you a full cup of medicine, sour medicines, stronger then your disease; and it can
8 cause you something again. Yeah.
9 I And did you ever go to a traditional healer yourself?
10 No I did not. I have never, no; maybe I will, but I don't think of doing that. Maybe I don't get ... I do feel
11 sick, but I just take aspirin, haha.
12 I Hmhm, but if for example that aspirin wouldn't help or if the doctor can't help, then you think
13 you might consider going to a traditional healer...
14 R It depends on the doctor I have consulted; yeah; you know, some of the doctors are not good, some of
15 them are good. Some of them are there for money and some of them are there for their own profession.
16 But I have never gone to a traditional healer, maybe I will, but I don't believe in them. Some of them
17 are just, they are just there to increase the pain of the patient. Because if you are given more medicine,
18 since your disease is not at all that serious. It can even be more serious because of that. For that I
19 feel afraid.
20 I Yeah, so it's you think they might give you too much because they don't have the skills to decide
21 how much they should give.
22 R Yah, yah.

In line 4 respondent 3 makes clear that he is not inclined to consult traditional healers: 'I don't believe in traditional healers' and 'I have never (gone to a traditional healer), no; maybe I will, but I don't think of doing that.' (line 10). One of the reasons he gives for his 'disbelief' is that he doubts the skills of these healers. He suggests, that traditional healers might give a wrong kind and especially wrong dosage of medicine (lines 5,7,17) because of which 'it can even be more serious because of that'. And this 'can cause you something again' (line 8). Thus the respondent puts forward the risks he perceives as reason to reject witchdoctors. In line 18 the respondent says that he feels afraid. When respondents express negative feelings like fear or discomfort in relation to ATR-practices and –beliefs, they make clear that they don't just debunk ATR, but that there is a personal interest at stake. This makes their problematising more convincing. When a conversation partner gives fear as justification for not doing or believing in something, one will be inclined to readily accept his or her claims, without further explanation and justification.

This extract shows how ATR-practices can not only be portrayed as nonsensical and superfluous but also as potentially harmful and risky. This way of accounting for non-involvement which respondents use can be called 'Pointing out Risks'. It is a problematising account which respondents use most frequently to traditional healing and witchcraft.

Although 'Showing Risk' is an account which convincingly problematises ATR, it appears that respondents who use this account do not necessarily and completely reject ATR practices and related beliefs. Notice how in extract 7, line 10 and 16, the respondent says he has never gone to a traditional *but* 'maybe I will'. Here this respondent leaves open the option that he will consult a witchdoctor in the future. Although both times he immediately undoes this suggestion by saying 'but I don't think of doing that' (line 10) and 'but I don't believe in them' (line 16). Before the respondent mentions the risks he perceives in consulting unskillful traditional healers, he gives another reason why he did not consult these healers; he does not 'suspect anyone to harm' him (line 4). In a later passage in the interview he explicitly says, when he is asked whether it would be possible that he gets sick because somebody bewitches him: 'That can be possible but I can not suspect anyone .... That can definitely happen because jealousy is everywhere.' Thus, his assertion 'I don't suspect anyone to harm me' can be read, as 'I don't suspect anyone to bewitch me'. The respondent attends to the possibility that in certain circumstances, namely when he suspects people to harm, or rather, to bewitch him, he might consult a witchdoctor.

Thus, when Christian Malawians reject ATR by pointing at perceived risks, which certain practices and beliefs would bring along, they don't totally exclude ATR-practices from their lives. Nor does it mean that they deny the reality of ATR-'beliefs', like witchcraft. Fear of witchcraft itself can even be used as argument to reject certain ATR-practices. One respondent, S, made it clear that he would not consult witchdoctors as he 'would not love to compete with someone who is bewitching me'.

It becomes clear now that respondents can reject ATR for reasons, which are rather practical and pragmatic rather then principle and ideological (see box 3).

> **Box. 3** 'Ideological' is a term which will return more frequently in this thesis. It is a problematic concept as different scholars conceptualise 'ideology' it in different ways. Frequently ideology is used in a negative sense, like for example Marxist ideology can be declared an erroneous, biased reflection of reality (personal communication, van Loosbroek, July 2001). In this thesis 'ideological' is not used in this negative sense. The meaning of 'ideological talk' is inspired by van der Zweerden's definition of ideology: "a possible function of a relative coherent set of theoretical claims and *practical valuations*, directed at the *organising of engagement and actions of the social group* and/or the legitimatisation of the status quo." [Italics added] (1994: 50).
> In this thesis, talk is called 'ideological' when respondents show to make judgements about what is good and bad for Malawian Christians or what Christians should do and should not do in order to strive for a worthy – in this case Christian - goal. By using ideological claims, respondents can p-osition themselves as Christians.

Sometimes respondents speak both in an ideological, moralizing and a pragmatic manner about ATR. See for example how in the next extract the respondent argues that he did not perform birth rituals on his children.

Extract 9 R1 6/10

1. I Hmhm, because ehh, I eh I heard that some people in Malawi that they have special birth-rites for if
2. children are born that they, I don't know exactly what they do then, but there are certain rituals which
3. they perform to make sure that the child is going to be okay or something..
4. R Ah no, my children I haven't done that, I have already said that I am a Christian, so I haven't because
5. we have the word of (God ?) that's it. We have the hospital, so there's no need we have what a ritual.
6. I Yeah. Hmhm
7. R I, ah that's not necessary. Because those rituals, sometimes, they kill

kids, they can say...the kid
8. suffers from let's say [malasmous....?] or malnutrition. Where they go by giving him traditional
9. medicine, which is not helpful to the kid. Definitely the kid will die! But if you go and go to the
10. hospital, they will say, oh, this one, the kid has such and such thing so I can give him such such,
11. because this medicine, it will work and it works! And that's the end of it. But eh if you go to tiny
12. villages, where the hospitals are just very far away. Yeah. They practice rituals.
13 R Yeah they are thinking that the kid will be okay, while they are giving it the wrong treatment. For
14. wrong disease.
15 Hmhm, mm, mm. But ehm, so is it then that, ehm, ja, hah (interviewer's reaction to wife of respondent).
16. So is then the most important reason why eh, your kids they didn't eh perform the
17. birth-rites, is that because you think they might harm the kids and it's not, they are making them
18. better, or you should go to a hospital or some place .and not...
20. R Because, if this tradition, ah, it's not good for a Christian. It's ( ) (joining?) this tradition. Because
21. some tradition it (seems), that's why I don't go to tradition, yeah

The first reason the respondent in extract 9 gives for not performing birth rituals with his children is that he is a Christian (line 4). He stresses this identity claim by saying he has 'already said' he is a Christian. As Christian he belongs to those who have the word of God, which is sufficient: 'That's it' (line 5). However, in the same line he adds another reason why there is 'no need' for birth rituals; 'we have the hospital'. Moreover, in line 9 the respondent makes clear that birth rituals are not only useless, but also dangerous and harmful. In lines 7-15 he elaborates on this pragmatic argument, and gives thereby the Perceived Risk argument more 'discursive' weight then the 'Christian' Legislative Rejection. Also strong wordings like 'Definitely the kid will die!' (line 9) and the respondent's exclaiming intonation make especially the Pointing out Risk-account convincing and important in the problematising of ATR. In lines 16-19 the interviewer provides a gist of the respondent's explanation in which she stresses the pragmatic nature.

However, in line 20 O does not attend to the interviewer's suggestion that pragmatic reasons are most important for O's rejection of birth rituals. Instead, he repeats his ideological claim, stressing that 'this tradition' is 'not good for a Christian' (line 20) and that that is the reason why he did not perform all.

More frequently 'Perceiving Risk'-accounts are accompanied by more ideological, principled, arguments like 'Christian Moralizing' and 'Legislative Rejection'. The latter accounts are often put forward first, and more prominently. Especially when the perceived risk has a supernatural nature, like witchcraft. In conversation with a white European researcher to reject ATR as immoral or unchristian is possibly considered a more justified account than to show a pragmatic rejection on the basis of fears of, for example witchcraft. In other words, Malawian Christians may consider especially an European white researcher as 'Christian Moralizing' and 'Legislative Rejection' as warranted accounts rather then 'Pointing out Risk'.

It will have become clear by now that using the account of 'Pointing out Risk' is a way of rejecting ATR which is in itself hardly related to Christianity. 'Perceiving Risk' is a conditional rejection of ATR: it is not that Christians by definition can't deal with ATR-practices and -beliefs, it's only better not to get involved in those practices and beliefs which bring along risks to personal well-being. Hence, being Christian is not always of relevance when explaining why one does not deal with ATR. Respondents using a mundane Perceiving Risk account make available the inference that getting involved in risky ATR-practices and beliefs may make someone a thoughtless, reckless person, but *not* that dual involvement makes someone a less sincere Christian.

Conclusion

The accounts 'Debunking'; and 'Pointing out Risk' which have been discussed in this section show that Malawian Christians do not only reject ATR for reasons which are related to Christianity. Respondents, who declare ATR nonsensical, primitive or harmful, don't directly reject ATR as 'evil' or 'unchristian'. Rejection of ATR by these accounts is not unconditional: respondents can leave open the option to deal with ATR-practices if necessary, or with those practices which are not useless and harmful. It appears that respondents don't always construct ATR and Christianity as oppositional categories.

Thus, Malawian Christians who use accounts like 'Debunking' and 'Pointing out Risk' engage in a practical kind of talk, rejecting ATR for pragmatic reasons. The respondents make relevant both pragmatic but and more ideological reasons when rejecting ATR-practices and beliefs. Hereby they position themselves as devoted Christian who therefore reject ATR-practices or –beliefs. In addition, Malawian Christians can engage in 'identity talk' when using accounts like 'Debunking' and 'Pointing out Risk', and position themselves as modern Malawians.

Another observation that is worth mentioning is that Malawian Christians can still attend to the reality of ATR-beliefs -like witches- while 'Debunking' or 'Pointing out Risk'.

Intermezzo II: The questions left unanswered

Several ways have been observed in which Christian Malawians reject ATR. Thus respondents can be said to subscribe to the rejecting stance of the Christian church. Yet, sometimes respondents reject ATR for reasons, which are not specifically Christian or even not related to Christianity at all. Apparently the Christian faith is not the only thing, which is relevant for rejecting or accepting ATR. This raises the question to what extent Malawian Christians have to reject ATR in order not to endanger their Christian identity-project. To what extent can Christian Malawians position themselves as Christian *without* rejecting ATR? These questions are related to another unravelled mystery; how is it possible that although respondents problematise ATR in several ways, they claim to be involved in ATR as well? There appear to be certain contradictions and ambiguities in what the Christian Malawian respondents do and say in relation to ATR. These contradictions call for explanation. The different ways in which Malawian Christians problematise ATR have already been charted. In order to come to an understanding of Malawian Christians' ambivalent accounting-practices, it might be fruitful to examine how Christian Malawians unproblematise ATR.

5.3 Unproblematising ATR: Identity- and pragmatic-talk

Christian Malawians must be doing quite some work to account in such a way for ATR-involvement of both themselves and compatriots that they can accept ATR-involvement, while leaving the ideological claim that ATR and

Christianity can not go together intact. As suggesting that Malawians are a friendly, tolerant people will not provide much insight in this issue; therefore some more concrete discursive interactions will be investigated. The purpose is to find out what kind of accounts Malawian Christians give which unproblematise ATR-involvement, and how these accounts function in Malawian Christians' discourse.

5.3.1 Unproblematising ATR: Externalization and Rationalization

Like with the different problematising accounts, also different types of accounts, which Christian Malawians use to condone, or unproblematise ATR can be discerned. In this section two kinds of accounts will be addressed. First, it will be shown how Christian Malawians can 'externalise' ATR-involvement, putting the cause for involvement outside themselves or 'others' who perform ATR. Second, a type of account will be discussed in which respondents 'rationalise' ATR-involvement, whereby they justify performing certain ATR practices or having certain traditional religious beliefs as logical and normal.

Situational coercion

Regularly respondents mention external factors, like demographic variables or certain life-situations, which can 'explain' why people are involved in ATR. For example they make clear that especially elderly want to perform funeral rites, or that initiations are normal in certain ethnic groups. Having a health problem, which is related to sexuality –being barren or having a sexually transmittable disease- or having bad social relations, are circumstances, which are associated with witchcraft. These circumstances can be put forward to justify the consulting of a witchdoctor, which is constructed as logical and inevitable in these situations.

The interviewer often pushes respondents to put forward certain variables by her questions, for example by asking whether certain people in Malawi deal with ATR (see appendix D). Hence, what's interesting is not *that* respondents put forward certain external, explanative factors, but *how* Christian Malawians *use* the demographic variables or other 'fixed givens' in their accounting-practices.[7]

By using the account 'Situational Coercion', respondents can construct different categories of people, who are living in their own coercive reality. They do this among others by frequently speaking about they and them: 'it's just them', 'it's their belief', while condoning other people's ATR-involvement. Respondents suggest hereby that it is unnecessary, or even impossible, to condemn ATR-involvement of people if you are not in the same coercive situation. Also in combination with other accounts, respondents often stress that ATR-involvement is everybody's own choice and own 'understanding'. Hereby respondents circumvent to explicitly condone or to explicitly condemn the involvement in ATR. Involvement in ATR of fellow Christians and fellow countrymen is presented as a trivial 'non-issue', not directly interfering with their being Christian.

Thus, by using accounts like 'Situational Coercion', respondents construct a 'reality', pertaining to certain situations, at certain moments in life, in which it is self-evident and rather inevitable that other people, or even they themselves, become involved in ATR. Certain people, in certain situations, can't help dealing with ATR; they just happen to live in an obtrusive ATR-reality.

Cultural coercion

Sometimes Christian Malawians talk about living in the Malawian society with its own specific culture as the 'situation', which forces them to deal with ATR.

Extract 10 R12 9/19

(Before the respondent talked quite elaborately about his consulting of traditional healers. He also explained why the church disapproves of Christians

---

[7] A difference between discourse analytic research and more traditional approaches in for example social psychology and sociology becomes clear here. In the latter approaches, demographic factors or life-situations will be considered as explanatory factor, useful for the calculation of correlations and regression-analysis. However, in this research, the extent to which these factor can explain variance is not of importance. What matters is how Christian Malawians themselves *use* these factors in their accounting-practices.

consulting traditional healers; the healers are associated with taking revenge and worshipping idols. It took some time before Mr. H mentioned the latter reason, which he introduced by saying 'oh well, and the other thing I have remembered. They always say...')

1. Ehm, the times that you went to a traditional healer, ehm, did you have in a way as well the feeling
2. then that you were worshipping an unchristian God as a Christian?
3. Yeah exactly, exactly. Especially at one occasion [tells that when sister was very sick they consulted
4. a traditional healer who has a goat which could speak] and I had the feeling that ah I am really
5. worshipping an idol, I had that feeling haha.
6. I   Hmhm, Okay
7. R   Yes
8. I   And what did you think about that, did you think okay but I should have to do it, I have to do it
9. I   because people are ill here or?
10. R   Yeah, I had to do it, I was forced because, ehm, as a sister, as a brother to the sister who was sick. I
11. I wouldn't say no, I don't want to do that. Because we had visited so many doctors and we didn't get
12. any help and so. And I wouldn't tell my mother, or my relatives to say no I can't go there, I can not
13. escort my sister there because I am a Christian believer. Then I would be thought of being a w (.)
14. perhaps a witch myself. So (.)
15. I   So you felt you had to, although you knew it was unchristian maybe in some way, but you felt you had to.
16. R   Yeah. So you know, you see now this culture now, is fighting against the Christianity. So, I was in
17. dilemma. I was in between two different worlds. So I was forced. I always, I I in that situation I am
18. always forced to our tradition.
19. I   Then you you would say if there's a possible conflict between your Christianity and your culture, then
20. you would say you would choose for your culture or.
21. R   Yeah.. I can, I can even choose for Christianity, but eh always is for the culture. Just because we are

22.		living in a community, in a cultural community.
22.	I	But always is for the culture you say?
23.	R	Not not always for the culture. You'll do, you'll do, judge the situation. As to this type of situation,
24.		which side should I choose. Is it the Christian side or the cultural side. So (.) But in most cases,
25.		especially where somebody is critically ill, you are always forced to follow the cultural (.) system.

In lines 3-5 the respondent problematises his consulting of a traditional healer by confirming the interviewer's suggestion that he had the feeling he visited an idol (line 4,5). This confirmation becomes extra convincing by the respondent's stressing intonation, and by his saying 'exactly, exactly' (line 3). From a western perspective, the respondent hereby creates an obligation for further accounting. For, if he really had the feeling to visit an idol why did he do it? However, the respondent does not attend to any need for further explanation. It is the interviewer who suggests in line 8 a 'solution,' which he readily confirms: he had to consult a witchdoctor because his sister was sick. The respondent justifies his ATR-practice by using an account, which can be called 'Cultural Worldview'. In this account the respondent constructs ' culture', or 'tradition', as an external force: *'So I was forced. I always, I I in that situation I am always forced to our tradition.'* (line 17). By using the words 'always' (line 17, 21) and 'just' (line 21) and emphasising the former, makes the obeying of culture self evident and inevitable.

The respondent makes it clear that in such a coercive situation being Christian is not considered a warranted account to reject the ATR-practice of consulting traditional healers. He does this in lines 12 and 13 when he says: 'And I wouldn't tell my mother, or my relatives to say no I can't go there, I can not escort my sister there because I am a Christian believer. Then I would be thought of being a w (.) perhaps a witch myself. So.' Here, the respondent anticipates a possible counterclaim that he could, or perhaps even should have refused to go to a traditional healer on grounds of being Christian. In the first lines of extract 10, the respondent makes clear that he did take into account his Christian identity while consulting the traditional healer. In the introduction of this thesis it was mentioned that scholars – especially non-Africans- frequently suspect that African Christians, who are dealing with two religions, experience some kind of religious 'schizophrenia'. However, the Christian Malawians who were interviewed for this research hardly ever mentioned such kind of psychological problems. They rather frequently show to consider dual religious involvement as taken for granted. Yet, the respondent does put effort to show that he really had the feeling 'that ah I am really worshipping an idol' (line 3) and that he was in a dilemma (line 16). Hereby he portrays himself as someone who was already during his consulting of the traditional healer considering that he was worshipping idols and did not feel right about it. This is somewhat remarkable as this respondent gave an elaborate account earlier in the interview about why and when it is useful to consult traditional healers and witchdoctors, and talked in detail about instances in which he consulted them himself. Moreover, as said before, it took some time before the respondent seemed to remember that 'the church believes that, when you contact people for you to know who has done this to you, you are worshipping idols'. The aim is not to judge whether the respondent 'truly' experienced or experiences conflicts or not. But it does appear to be problematic to take the Cultural Coercion and accompanying 'dilemma' at face value, as reflection of 'real' motivations or other psychological constructs. It will be more fruitful to see the claims about 'stings of consciousness' as a rhetorical device to unproblematise and justify his ATR-involvement, contributing to the work of the cultural coercion account. By making clear that he did not feel happy to consult traditional healers, H convinces himself that it was really his culture and the situation he found himself in which forced him to consult traditional healers, and that he did not do this out of 'free will'. By referring Christianity and by stressing the dilemma he found himself in (lines 16,17), H positions himself as someone who is, although he has broken the church rules, a conscientious and devoted Christian. Note that the respondent speaks in abstract terms like 'cultural community', 'Christianity' and 'cultural system'. As noted before, this abstract, ideological way of talking – called 'identity talk' – accompanies the working up of one's Christian identity.

It is noteworthy to see that the respondent makes clear that it was not merely because he had to abide by the cultural values that he consulted the witchdoctor. In line 13 he casually gives a less ideological and more pragmatic argument: he would run the risk of being accused of being a witch. Again, witchcraft appears to be a relevant, readily available resource for Malawians who are accounting in social interactions.

'Cultural Coercion' is not only used as externalisation- but also as rationalisation or normalisation-device. Regularly Christian Malawian respondents speak about typically Malawian ways of interpreting of and acting in the world, which are considered normal in Malawi. For example, some respondents stress that in general, Malawians tend to associate every unexpected death with witchcraft. Respondents also stress that feelings of jealousy are abundant in Malawi, and that this is a major cause of witchcraft. Hereby respondents normalise 'believing' in witchcraft typical for Malawians, and make it logical that in case Malawians get arguments they consult a witchdoctor. Christian Malawians who use this account show to adhere to a way of interpreting and acting which is logical and not idiosyncratic and contingent. Respondents construct worldviews as generally valid, 'logical' and self-evident by speaking in general terms like 'we Malawians believe' or 'they think'. By emphasising that the cultural worldview belongs to Malawi, to '*ou*r traditional culture *here*', respondents make their claims generally valid –for all Malawians- but at the same time also specific: they only pertain to Malawians. By putting forward 'Cultural Coercion', Malawian Christians make clear that they have a way of doing, thinking and interpreting which differs from the white, European interviewer's frame of reference. The interviewer is positioned –to some extend already from the start of the interview of course- as the 'apprentice' who is to accept it as fact what her 'teachers', the respondents, tell her. Hence, the interviewer is pressed to accept as 'fact' that certain ATR-practices and –beliefs are normal and self-evident in Malawi, which safeguards the Malawian respondent from being criticised for engaging in ATR.

Sometimes respondents carry their 'Cultural Coercion' account somewhat further. Some cultivate a commitment to their culture and claim that one should be proud of one's culture and one should not forsake it. Hereby they justify or unproblematise ATR-involvement as something which is not only acceptable but even respectable. Especially highly educated people and clergy use this form of 'Cultural Coercion'. The inculturation-policy of the Roman Catholic Church, which calls upon Malawians to bring their culture into the church, is the institutionalised form of this cultural coercion account.

Another way in which respondents normalise ATR-involvement by 'Cultural Coercion' is by pointing out the utility of certain 'cultural' ideas or practices, for example, when respondents explain that the funeral-custom of cutting hair is meant to prevent that the dead start haunting their living family members. Or that children are taught useful, necessary things at initiation. As has been mentioned in the outline of the analytical perspective, in functionalistic theories in the social sciences, functions of behaviour are put forward to explain the occurrence of certain practices. However, from a discourse analytic, cultural psychological perspective, it's problematic to explain behaviour with such functions. Especially not when they are deduced from interview-data in which respondents clearly ad hoc and in retrospect construct possible functions of ATR-practices. What should be studied is how this attributing of a function 'functions' itself. By showing that ATR-aspects are not only common but, on top of that, useful for society or for its individuals, it becomes normal or even inevitable to perform ATR-practices and to have certain ATR-beliefs as member of this society. If a Malawian Christian explains that children are taught things about sexuality and procreation at initiation, one understands more easily that parents send their children to initiation, especially when respondents add that Malawians are shy to tell their children themselves about sexuality. Thus, by pointing out functions or the utility of behaviour, individuals can justify it, like performing certain ATR-practices. Meanwhile, it should again be noted that while pointing out functions of ATR, Malawian Christians attend to and thereby construct the reality of ATR-'beliefs'. For instance, when one points out that a ritual like cutting hair is useful for preventing the dead from bothering people, at that moment one orients to and constructs the reality of dead people being able to haunt the living.

Obeying Others

Besides life-situations and their culture, Christian Malawians also put forward concrete people in their social environment as external forces, who 'drag' people into ATR. Respondents regularly assert that they performed a practice because their friends, parents or elderly wanted them to. Respect for parents and elderly is often said to be an important value in African countries. So, can be concluded that Christian Malawians put forward others as cause for their ATR-involvement because they don't want to be deemed disrespectful members of society who don't follow the norm of respecting other people like elderly? In a discourse analytic study as this one, one should be careful not to reify cultural values and use it as explanatory factor for people's involvement in ATR. More detailed analysis is required of conversational interactions in which Christian Malawian respondents refer to others in relation to their or other's ATR involvement. Respondent 11 did not perform birth rituals for her children. In the next extract, she explains why and how she managed not to perform those rites.

Extract 11 R11 7/16

1. I   Yeah yeah. And were such kind of things done with your children as well?
2. R   No, no just coming from the hospital that was it.
3. I   Hm, and, why not?
4. R   Yeah because, for me I don't think it will get medicines. Maybe because I have spend my life in UK
5. (like that?). So it's like what I was saying is that the children may once they are born they have never
6. taken place anything (like going to the graveyard ...?) So I was saying no I think I'll leave my children
7. just like those because I want to see what is going to happen.(And then again ...did happen?).
8. I   Jaja hm, and
9. R   might expect, bad people were saying that once some people, bad people hear, don't actually
10. (happen) protected them, you know they do something bad. So I said why should I
11. (practicize/publicise?) it, my children, I don't want them to do this. That's enough.
12. I   Jaja aha, so you thought why should, I don't have to tell everyone that I didn't do it, [so (.)
13. [No actually there
14. was no need, it was, it's not, what happens is that, once you see the name in this (it's just ...) these
15. people are doing traditional things. But then it's nowadays I think mostly people
16. do that, you know, not many people.
17. I   Hmhm, but was it also then that you thought if I, if no-one, I don't have to tell anyone that we didn't
18. do those traditional things, and if no-one knows then they can't eh bewitch us because we (.)
19. R   No , because what happens, what normally happens once you have given birth. ((tells that people from
20. the village come and 'bring those things'. You receive them but 'tell them
21. no, I'll do this later' I Yahyah

22. R   And you just make them happy when you receive it to show them that, (.) you have done, you are sort
23. of abiding by their standards. So that at least you should lower yourself to their standing. You
24. shouldn't, because once you don't accept this, okay she thinks she is higher. That's where witchcraft
25. comes in.

The respondent in extract 11 rejects the ATR-practice of performing birth rituals (line 2) by saying, ' *No, no just* coming from the hospital, *that was it*'. By using the word 'just' and 'that was it', she constructs visiting the hospital as mundane and normal. In line 4, she relates her not performing birth rituals to her stay in the UK. Hereby the respondent 'debunks' the practice as belonging to people who have had less European or western experiences. However, the respondent explains that she did not show other people that she did not perform birth rituals. In lines 17-18 she advises what is best to do in such a situation; to accept 'things' which people bring, pretend to use them, but throw them away when the people from the village are gone. In lines 20-21 the respondent tells the reason for pretending to accept the gifts 'you should lower yourself to their standing" and by receiving 'you just make them happy'. She makes clear that it is not, or not only, because of respect towards fellow Malawians that she advises to act in accordance with traditional customs. In line 9-10 she says that 'bad people' might 'do something bad'. The respondent points out that not accepting will make people think you are conceited: 'okay she thinks she is higher', and 'that's where witchcraft comes in.' (line 24). Thus, the respondent makes relevant witchcraft to explain and justify the way she manoeuvred between rejecting and accepting ATR. The way the respondent orients to witchcraft in her accounting, shows as well that even when respondents reject ATR, they can still attend to the reality of ATR-'beliefs'.

It can be concluded that 'Obeying Others' is an account by which respondents make clear that there can be concrete others in their lives who force them to deal with ATR. When respondents stress that they perform ATR because they have to obey others, they externalise the cause of their ATR-involvement and make clear they are involuntarily involved in ATR. Thereby they position themselves as Malawian Christians who might deal with ATR but are not intrinsically motivated for ATR-practices and –beliefs. By using 'Obeying Others', respondents can claim to perform ATR-practices or to have ATR-beliefs while still on principal rejecting Christians ATR-involvement. Thus 'Obeying Others' is an account, which Christian Malawians use for justifying and thus unproblematising the performing of ATR-practices.

It has become clear that 'Obeying Others' justifying function does not exactly work as would be expected from a western point of view. Christian Malawians don't only obey others to comply with the 'cultural value' of showing respect. In extract 11 it can be observed how a more pragmatic reason is put forward; not performing ATR involves a risk of being bewitched. Apparently, claiming to fear witchcraft is a socially accepted justification for performing, or pretending to perform ATR. It becomes clear once more that witchcraft is a self-evident reality for Malawians. Another important finding is that analysis of the way the account 'Obeying Others' is used shows again that Christian Malawians can account for ATR-involvement without referring to Christianity and their Christian identity. Malawian Christians don't always contrast ATR-practices with Christian practices; they can contrast them with modern practices as well, or don't contrast ATR at all. Again, it becomes clear that Malawian Christians, when accounting for ATR, are able to engage in different kinds of talk: besides a more ideological kind of 'identity talk', they can engage in a more pragmatic kind of 'practical talk'.

Risk Reducing

Another (pragmatic) account which respondents use to unproblematise ATR-involvement by rationalising it is what can be called 'Risk Reducing'. In chapter 5 it has been explained that ATR-practices and –beliefs can be rejected by putting forward risks for one's well being which certain ATR-practices would bring along. On the other hand, respondents frequently point out that people can perform ATR-practices if they reduce certain risks and are beneficial for ones well being. Like one respondent said when asked whether Christians could go to traditional healers: 'Yes, provided they get healed'. The unproblematising account 'Risk Reducing' is used especially in relation to traditional healing and birth rituals. The risk that has to be reduced can both be natural and supernatural. An example of the former is when birth rituals are said to make babies' fontanels stronger. Birth rituals pertain to supernatural risks when they are considered to be prevention against witchcraft. Sometimes respondents allege that they only condone ATR-practices, which are related to natural protection. This does not mean

> **Box. 3** 'Ideological' is a term which will return more frequently in this thesis. It is a problematic concept as different scholars conceptualise 'ideology' it in different ways. Frequently ideology is used in a negative sense, like for example Marxist ideology can be declared an erroneous, biased reflection of reality (personal communication, van Loosbroek, July 2001). In this thesis 'ideological' is not used in this negative sense. The meaning of 'ideological talk' is inspired by van der Zweerden's definition of ideology: "a possible function of a relative coherent set of theoretical claims and *practical valuations*, directed at the *organising of engagement and actions of the social group* and/or the legitimisation of the status quo." [Italics added] (1994: 50).
>
> In this thesis, talk is called 'ideological' when respondents show to make judgements about what is good and bad for Malawian Christians or what Christians should do and should not do in order to strive for a worthy –in this case Christian - goal. By using ideological claims, respondents can position themselves as Christians,

that they reject the reality of supernatural entities like witches and ancestral sprits.

By showing to condone ATR-practices if they reduce risks for ones well being respondents show to tolerate only a specific kind of ATR-practices. As they thereby distinguish between better and worse kinds of ATR respondents position themselves as critical Christian Malawians who don't just blindly approve of all ATR-practice and believes. It is a discursive device to unproblematise ATR-involvement, at least in certain practices or beliefs. Thereby they unproblematise their condoning of certain ATR-practices.

5.3.2 Unproblematising ATR: Trivialisation

Malawian Christians do not only engage in externalisation and rationalisation to justify ATR-involvement. In this paragraph some extracts will be discussed in which they unproblematise ATR-involvement.

Historiography

When discussing accounts which problematise ATR, it was already mentioned that sometimes respondents engage in historiography'. Hereby they construct ATR as a historical relic, belonging to the past. This historiography can lead to a negative construction of ATR as backward, and primitive. Yet, extract 12 will show that respondents don't only use the account 'Historiography' to problematise ATR.

Extract 12 6-22 r1

1   I   Jaja, I see by time...hmhm. But so then at that moment that your friend went to go to that traditional
2   healer,. or, did you both think like yeah you should try this traditional healer, or...
3   R   No, he told me that ah I am going to such such person and I said 'Okay I 'll [help???] with you, can I
4   accompany you so that I can see for myself for what is done there'
5   I   Aha, you were curious...
6   R   But, but, you know what is happening, for our church, the Presbyterian, and most of the churches they
7   are against the traditional healing. So to me anyway, because by that time I was not, I didn't go, much
8   into Christianity.
9   I   You didn't go what?
10 R   I said, by the time I was going there, ya I was just going slow in Christianity. But as of now, how I
11 have seen the Christianity I don't think that you should go.
12 I   Aha, aha
13 R   Yah
14 I   And now you are more active and you think that people shouldn't go to those people.
15 R   Yah yah to those people, because prayer, prayer is enough.

In line 3 the respondent asserts that he accompanied a friend to a traditional healer. In line 7 he shows that he is aware that his church does not approve of this ATR-practice. Hereby he creates the obligation to account for his assertion that he went to the traditional healer himself that he does -spontaneously- in line 8. He creates a contrast between what he was doing his 'condition' in the past and nowadays: 'by that time', he 'was going slow in Christianity', whereas, in contrast, 'as of now, how I have seen the Christianity I don't think that you should go' (line 11). The respondent unproblematises his own ATR-involvement by making clear that it was something which he did in the past, and will not do anymore as he has gained insights into Christianity: 'how I have seen the Christianity'. The account, which O gives here, can be called 'Historiography'. Extract 12 shows that engaging in 'historiography' can be used to unproblematise one's ATR-involvement by referring it to a 'safe' place in the past, thereby pre-empting that one is sanctioned for it. In lines 12 and 16 O shows to adhere to the rejective stance of the church now by using a Legislative Rejection account, thereby constructing Christianity as Superior. He trivialises what he did in the past by showing that he has changed, and positions himself as someone who is now a devoted Christian who thinks that 'prayer is enough'.

It can be concluded that by using 'Historiography', Malawian Christians can justifiably claim to have performed certain ATR-practices or to have had certain ATR-'beliefs', while at the same time problematising this ATR-involvement. Their 'historiography' constructs the ATR-involvement as something which belongs to another era and which can't be sanctioned anymore. Malawian Christians use 'Historiography' to show that they have changed and position themselves as individuals who are devoted Christians now.

What is interesting is that although Malawian Christians can 'ban' ATR-practices and believes to the past, this does not mean that they totally ban the reality of ATR-beliefs and practices as well. For example, one respondent (respondent 5), rejected birth rituals as irrelevant and belonging to the past. At the same time she claimed that they did help to prevent her baby from being harmed by other women when she performed this ritual several years ago.

Superficial Interest

In extract 12 the respondent points out that he accompanied his friend 'to see for himself what is done there' (line 5). Hereby he immediately makes clear that, unlike the interviewer suggested, he did not go because he thought himself that his friend should go to the traditional healer. More frequently, respondents emphasise that they, or others, have been involved in ATR for 'superficial' reasons like curiosity. For example respondent 11 explained that she attended initiation because she was 'exited' and wanted 'to see what happened'. Putting forward" Superficial Interest is a way to trivialise ATR-involvement. By using 'Superficial Interest' respondents show they are no 'hardcore' ATR-performers who are convinced of ATR reality and usefulness. However, they don't say that they do not accept an ATR-reality.

Respondents construct their ATR-involvement as 'not really' ATR-involvement, or at least as not the ATR involvement, which the church disapproves of. This unproblematising account which is also used as criterion to condone ATR-involvement of others: for example, respondents state that as long as you go to initiation just to watch, it is no problem to attend this traditional practice.

Conclusion

Different types of unproblematising accounts can be discerned: 'Situational Coercion', 'Cultural Coercion', 'Obeying Others' and 'Risk Reducing'. Christian Malawians use these discursive devices to externalise the cause of their ATR-involvement. They construct –together with the interviewer- a reality in which they are more or less helpless with regard to ATR. Christian Malawians can convince a 'judging audience' that *in certain situations* – which do not have to be more specific then living in Malawi- one has to believe in, or practice, ATR. Being a Christian does not change this coercive ATR-reality at and is not of enough relevance, or not of relevance at all, for deciding whether or not to turn to ATR in those situations. In addition, respondents use the unproblematising accounts to rationalise ATR-involvement: they make clear that *in certain situations* it is logical and normal to be involved in ATR. By using these unproblematising devices, respondents can claim to perform in certain situations, certain ATR-practices, or to hold certain ATR-beliefs, and at the same time that on principle ATR and Christianity can not go together. Thus respondents can show to be involved in ATR and still position themselves as devoted Christians, committed to their faith.

Not always can unproblematising respondents be perceived to put effort in positioning themselves as devoted Christians. Sometimes they engage in *practical* talk, pointing out pragmatic benefits of ATR without making relevant any possible conflicts with Christianity.

In addition, it has been observed that in certain instances Malawian Christians trivialise ATR-involvement when talking to a white researcher about ATR. Malawian Christians can make clear by 'Historiography' that they 'only' performed ATR in the past and by 'Superficial Interest' that they got involved in ATR for superficial reasons. ATR-involvement is depicted as too trivial to be discussed, let alone to sanction Christians for it. Whereas the interviewer tries to discover whether there is not anything problematic for

Christians to be involved in ATR, the respondents turn ATR-involvement into an unimportant 'non-issue'

Respondents who engage in trivialising can admit that they performed certain ATR-practices or that they have certain beliefs -or at least don't reject them- but make clear that they are no 'hardcore' ATR-performers and believers. Hereby trivialising Malawian Christians can admit ATR-involvement and still position themselves as devoted Christians. They can even claim that ATR and Christianity cannot go together.

Intermezzo III: The questions left unanswered

So far, we have seen that Malawian Christians problematise in different ways different ATR-practices and beliefs, and that they regularly do this by making relevant Christian arguments. They show that ATR-practices and beliefs are not something for Christians to engage in. At the same time the interviewed Christians do show to be involved in ATR. This raised the question how Christian Malawians can both reject ATR, *and* still be involved in it. Looking more closely at the problematising accounts it appeared that respondents do not always refer to Christianity and their Christian identity when problematising ATR. Sometimes they position themselves as modern and critical persons when putting forward arguments to reject ATR. In addition, sometimes problematising accounts have a very pragmatic nature, as they are related to 'mundane' protection of personal well-being. This suggested that Malawian Christians can engage in ATR while preserving a sincere Christian 'identity'. It became clear that indeed, Malawian Christians not only problematise but also unproblematise ATR in talk with a western researcher. Respondents construct certain forms of ATR-involvement as not interfering with Christian commitment. Several discursive techniques can be discerned which Malawian Christians use to engage in justified, intelligible talk about own or other's ATR-involvement. By 'externalisation' respondents put the cause of ATR-involvement outside themselves. By 'rationalisation' they make ATR-involvement logical and normal, and by 'trivialisation' they construct ATR-involvement as coincidental and superficial and thus not important enough to be addressed as in some way problematic

As all ATR-aspects which have been addressed in the interviews, are both problematised and unproblematised -although certain ATR-aspects are more problematised than others- Malawian Christians account in an ambivalent way for ATR-involvement. They both say yes and no to ATR. Charting the different types of accounts, which Christian Malawians give, does not give sufficient insight in this specific accounting-pattern. It leaves open the question why Christian Malawians don't just either straightforwardly accept or reject ATR. This is a controversial question in discourse analysis, as one is inclined to answer why-questions in terms of 'real' forces or motivations outside discourse. Discourse analysts refrain by definition form such causal explanations. However, from within a discourse analytic and cultural psychological perspective, the question can be posed how Christian Malawians manage to *both* problematise *and* unproblematise ATR. By answering this question we can come to an understanding in underlying interactional mechanisms, which generate the ambivalent accounting-pattern, which has been discerned.

6. Christianity and ATR: Of a Different Order, at Different Levels

So far we have seen that Christian Malawian respondents account for ATR in an ambivalent way; they both say yes and no to their ATR-practices and –beliefs. In order to gain more insight into the reproduction of this ambivalent accounting-pattern, in this chapter special attention will be paid to those interview extracts, which strike as ambivalent, contradictory and paradoxical.

6.1 Attending to ATR-'beliefs': Ambivalence, contradiction and paradox

So far we have already seen that when *unproblematising*, but even when *problematising* different ATR-practices and –beliefs, Christian Malawians attend to and construct the reality of supernatural entities like witches and ancestral spirits. In most respondents acknowledged this 'ATR-reality' implicitly. How do Malawian Christians orient themselves to the ATR-'beliefs' when the western interviewer directly asks about them?

Extract 13 R56 10/17

1. I I heard that sometimes in Malawi people can bewitch each other, that there are witches
2. RL: Oh yes, there are some witches, yes.
3. I They, they exist.
4. (nonverbal confirmation?)

Extract 14 R7 9/18

(respondent talked about ancestral spirits)
1. I But, but, but, they are there?
2. R They are there!, I am sure, they are there. And they come to you through this type of coming. With
3. I somebody who starts shouting or doing this and that.

Extract 15 R12 10/3

1. I Jaja, ja. Ehm another thing I was wondering, ehm I've heard some people telling abou
2. R ancestral spirits, eh I think you also mentioned it earlier. Ehm do you, would you say that there ar
   I ancestral spirits?
3. R Yes.
4. I Hmhm
5. R I believe there are ancestral spirits. And eh, ehm, yah I have got an experience myself.
6.   (some lines omitted in which respondent talks about the experience of the ancestral spirit)
7. I Hmhm, okay. But you <u>would</u> say that there are ancestral spirits?
8. R Yeah I would say so. Because what makes me feel there are ancestral spirits is that <u>myself</u> I have met
9 .   several of them on the road, during night. At home.

In extract 13 the respondent confirms the existence of witches. Her answer is of a causal nature, especially because of her words 'Oh yes' and 'some' (line 2). Also in extracts 14 and 15 the respondents give straightforward confirmations in response to the interviewer's question whether there are ancestral spirits. In extract 14 the confirmation is not only straightforward but also emphatic due to the repetition of the phrase 'they are there' (line 2), the exclaiming intonation (line 3) and because the respondents qualifies his reality claim as certain: 'I am sure'. In both extract 14 and 15 the respondents account for their statement that there are ancestral spirits by engaging in what Edwards and Potter (1992) call "empiricist accounting." Both respondents refer to ways in which ancestral spirits can be experienced. In extract 15 the respondent accounts for the existence of ancestral spirits by saying: 'Yeah I would say so. *Because* what makes me feel there are ancestral spirits is that <u>myself</u> I have met several' (line 8). He 'proves' his belief in ancestral spirits with personal experiences: ancestral spirits exist, because he himself has noticed that they exist. By such empiricist accounts, respondents construct the reality of supernatural entities like spirits, thus backing up their reality claim.

Besides empiricist accounting respondents use reference to media reports to convincingly argue for the reality of certain ATR-beliefs. They mention newspapers, radio, and television reports of instances of witchcraft, rain withholding[8] and the like as 'proof'. The media are used as authoritative source about the truth of the 'reality of ATR'. If even the newspapers[9] write about witchcraft, it must be real!

Thus, also when the western researcher directly asks Malawian Christians after their 'belief' in supernatural entities like witches and ancestral spirits, Malawian Christians construct these entities as irrefutably real. This is somewhat surprising: how can for example such a reality claim be reconciled with the biblical commandment 'thou shalt not abide idols'?

Indeed the next extracts show that claiming the existence of ancestral spirits or witchcraft is not completely unproblematic. In the extracts 16 and 17 I will point out three different, but interrelated issues. First, in both extracts I will show how the expressing of ignorance about a certain phenomenon – witches, spirits- points at the problematic nature of this phenomenon and functions as a way to distance oneself from it. Second, I will use the extracts to make clear that reality claims about ATR-entities are often ambivalent. Third, I will point at a difference between believing in and claiming existence, as constructed by Christian Malawians talking about dual religious involvement.

Note that extract 16 is the continuation of extract 13 in which the respondent straightforwardly acknowledged the existence of witches. The respondent of extract 17 is the same as the one who emphatically acclaimed the reality of ancestral spirits in extract 14.

Extract 16 R56 10/17 (ex. 13 continued)

1. I   I heard that sometimes in Malawi people can bewitch each other, that there are witches (.)
2. RL   Oh yes, there are some witches, yes.
3. I   They they exist
4.   (nonverbal confirmation?)
5. I   Did you experience that sometimes?
6. RL   We just hear that someone has been bewitched. Aha.

---

[8] See the ethnographic description in chapter 4

[9] Appendix F shows that newspapers do report about events related to ATR-practices and beliefs. Hereby they often depict ATR-beliefs as factual, although they are sometimes contended as well.

7.	I	And then people get sick, or what happens then? How do you know someone is bewitched?
8.	RL	hahaha. I think it is just a belief, yes.
9.	I	But for example if you ehm if you become ill at a certain day, and someone says to you you are
10.		bewitched, ehm what would you say or do, or?
11.	RL	hahaha
12.	RJ	For me I don't believe to that
13.	I	You don't what?
14.	RL	believe
15.	RJ	don't believe.
17.	RL	Because a witchdoctor can die. And I can die. Anyone can die. So to me it's just, it means it is, I think
18.		it is pagan to say this woman is a witchdoctor. You don't know. You can't see a witch. Yeah. Hahaha.
19.	I	So there are no witches, or are there?
20.	RL	You have some, there is witches or not yeah.
21.	RJ	(they/I ?) don't believe.
22.	I	So there are not. Or you don't know or (.) haha.
23.	RL	ah, just we don't bother. Whether there are witches or not. Yeah. We don't bother.
24.	I	Because is it then, ehm, there might be witches, but because you don't believe, it doesn't matter for
25.		you?
26.	RL	hmhm it matters. Haha. It does not matter, it matters not.
26.	I	And if someone would say that he does belief in witches, ehm, can that person be bewitched then?
27.	RL	Perhaps if he she believes she can bewitched or not. But my side I don't believe in witches yeah. A
28.		witch can die. Hahaha.
29.	I	A witch can die, then she is no witch anymore.
30.	RL	ah, yes no witch anymore
31.	I	But before she died she was a witch, or?
32.	RL	hahahahaha
33.	RL	Is is, that then, do you think that ehm you don't believe in witches because they don't have a lot of
34.		power because they can die, but before the died they <u>are</u> a witch and can harm people or can't they?
35.	RJ	I don't believe that there is witches because I have never seen them. Yeah. So I can't believe that.

36.	I	jaja
37.	RL	hahaha
38.	I	You don't think witches exist because you didn't experience it yourself.
39.	RL	We say she is a hooligan because I have seen him with walking with boys or women or men. Yeah
40.		you say that man be hooligan. But witch, I have never seen.
41.	RJ	I have never seen ( )
42.	RL	But a witch, you can't, you don't know that that person is a witch. Yes.

Extract 17 R7

1. And you don't think for example, I don't know, that that combination then of the bamboo and the heat
2. that that evokes a kind of magic power, which also like a kind of God changes scientifically the winds
3. and all that whereby the rain comes?
4. R   I don't think so. They work on coincidence. I don't know sometimes maybe they'll relate it to God. Our
5. God may not work in a favourable way. It is a coincidence that will make people be believers on
6. something which is just done on a trial basis or because they have heard or somebody told them.
7. You said they say our Gods=
8. R   =Hmhm, and which Gods I don't know. Haha. Which Gods they are talking about…Maybe the Gods
9. which accept the philosophy of (basking?) up an axe against a fire which may stop rain. Which Gods
10. I don't know.
11. I   It couldn't be a Christian God?
12. R   No, no, no. Usually when people say our Gods, they mean, they mean, the spirits of their forefathers.

In line 2 of extract 16, the respondent confirms the interviewer's suggestion that there are witches in Malawi. By taking her turn quickly and spontaneously -the interviewer does not explicitly ask a question- and by her words 'oh yes', J constructs the existence of 'some witches' as a self evident and mundane reality. Yet, when asked about personal experiences with witches, J distances herself from her reality-claim (line 6). She makes clear that she does not have experiences but that she 'just' heard that 'someone' has been bewitched.

> **Box. 4** Turn-taking is a central feature of conversation, which is intensively studied in conversation analysis. The norm in conversation is that only one party talks at a time. Therefore there are different 'turn-constructional' and 'speaker-selection principles' by which conversation-partners adhere to and reproduce this norm (Sacks, Schlegloff & Jefferson, in Moerman, 1988). "Overlap" is a term, which refers to moments when the second speaker starts speaking, whereas the first speaker has not yet finished his or her sentence, or "turn", in conversation. Moerman (1988) points out that overlap may seem to be a brake down of conversation's order, it frequently is the ordered product of interactive processes. Overlap is not just a sign of hampering conversation, a result of a conversation-partner not paying attention. Frequently it is not careless collision, but "pinpoint bombing" (Moerman, 1988:21).

The respondents in extract 16 make clear to have no experience with and no knowledge about witches. They do this first of all by avoiding several times to provide concrete information about witchcraft, requested by the interviewer. In line 6 the interviewer asks about the consequences of witchcraft, and about how one can know that someone has been bewitched. In response L laughs and asserts that 'it's just a belief' (line 8). Hereby she trivialises witchcraft and does not answer the question. Also in lines 11 and 12 the respondents do not answer the interviewer's question about what they would do or say when it would be suggested that they fell ill because of witchcraft: L laughs and J remarks 'For me I don't believe in that'. In line 21 the interviewer asks whether there are no witches or whether the respondents don't know. By the response 'ah we just don't bother. Whether there are witches or not' J and L are 'not answering', which makes available inferences like the respondents' unwillingness or inability to discuss witchcraft issues in some detail. In addition, like in line 8, the respondents' response trivialises witchcraft.

In addition, the respondents show lack of experience and knowledge in a more explicit way in lines 35 and 41. Here, J states not to believe in witches because she has never seen them. Moreover, in lines 18 and 42 the respondent make clear that one cannot know, nor see whether someone is a witch: 'You don't know. You can't see a witch.' (line 18). Hereby the make clear that it is unlikely that they will ever gain experiential knowledge about witches.

In this extract 16 J and L claim disbelief in witches and position themselves as people who have no knowledge about, experience with or interest in witches –they 'don't bother' (line 23) and 'it does not matter' (line 25). The respondents engage here in a type of accounting which can be called 'Foreclosing Ignorance', the function of which can be well explained in the basis of extract 17 where the 'Foreclosing Ignorance' account is more prominently present.

In extract 17 the respondent suggests that people who perform rain rituals 'relate it to God' (line 4). He does this in a delayed, cumbersome way by inserting 'don't know', 'sometimes' and 'maybe'. By this phrasing the respondent comes across as ignorant about the beliefs of people who perform rain rituals. He repeats his ignorance about the exact details of the rain rituals twice, in lines 8 and 9-10: 'which Gods I don't know', whereby he stresses that he is a person who is not knowledgeable about rain rituals. It is remarkable how quickly the respondent makes clear that he does not know *'Which Gods they are talking about...'*. Notice that in line 8, he takes over the interviewer's 'turn' by speaking before she has finished her sentence. The respondent immediately interprets the words *'You said they say our Gods...'* as leading to the question to which Gods the rain calling-people refer.

The conversational event in lines 7 and 8 is an example of 'latching', in which the second turn starts immediately after the first. The respondent's way of taking his turn comes across as what Moerman (1988) called 'pin-point bombing' (see Box 3), although Moerman used this in relation to moments of overlap in a conversation. In line 12 it becomes clear that the respondent's utterance of ignorance is not merely a sign of factual ignorance, as he appears to be more knowledgeable than he suggests before. When the interviewer wonders whether the Gods of people who perform this ritual might not be a Christian God (line 11), he immediately strongly corrects her: 'No, no, no.' (line 12) This denial is stressed by repeating it three times. Unlike in lines 8-10 the respondent now makes relevant knowledge rather than ignorance about the 'Gods': they are *not* Christian, and moreover he claims to know of which kind they are, namely 'the spirits of their forefathers.'(Line 12)

The expressing of ignorance can be related to Wooffitt's (1998) 'not naming device' and seems to serve a similar function. Wooffitt (op cit.) has pointed out that not naming can have a function in discourse, as naming implies knowledge about and interest in the phenomenon, which is named.

In addition, naming acknowledges an in-principle existence of the named object. Claiming ignorance about ATR-issues is a way to forestall inferences like being interested, convinced of their existence or believing in them. By providing a 'Foreclosing Ignorance' account, respondents can distance themselves from it, forestalling association with and being criticised for it. In extract 17 –and also at other moments in other interviews- 'I don't know' does not strike as neutral and factual, but rather as a commandment not to enquire any further. It is as if the respondent says 'I don't *want* to know, and I don't want to get involved'. And, moreover; 'I don't want you to think I know.' In extract 17 this distancing from ancestral spirits is sustained by the respondent's ridiculising in line 8, when he laughs after professing ignorance. In addition, in line 11 the respondent explicitly speaks about '*their* forefathers' whereby he distances himself from the Gods in which other people belief.

Also in extract 16 the professing of no knowledge about and experience with witches is a way to foreclose that the conversation partner inquires further about ATR. Thereby they forestall that they are identified as persons who are involved in ATR to such extent that they are judged as 'unchristian' or 'backward'. Note that in line 18 of extract 16 L says 'I think it is pagan to say this woman is a witchdoctor.' Hereby she relates identifying someone as a witch, with being pagan. Thus, by making clear they have never identified someone as witch – moreover by convincing their conversation-partner it is highly unlikely that they ever will, as they 'have *never* seen' (line 44), '*can't* know' (line 52) and 'don't bother whether there are witches or not' (line 23)- J and L position themselves as *not* pagans, or Christians.

I would now like to turn to the issue of ambivalence in the accounts about reality of and belief in ATR-entities. First, it should be noted that respondents using a 'Foreclosing Ignorance' account don't argue that supernatural entities and powers are non-existent. For example, also the respondent of extract 17 expresses 'belief' in the existence of ancestral spirits, which we have seen in extract 14. This suggests again that rather than taking an ignorance claim at face value, as 'truly' reflecting lack of knowledge, detailed investigation is required of the specific moment and specific way in which ignorance claims are used in talk-in-interaction, and of the function this specific use may serve.

Second, the claim of the respondents in extract 16 (lines 12, 15) that they don't believe in witches strikes, from a western perspective, as contradictory to L's spontaneous remark in line 2 that 'there are some witches'. Moreover, the respondents' arguing strikes as paradoxical. In line 17 L says, what can be taken as explanation for her not believing in witches that 'a witch can die'. In line 30 she confirms the interviewer's suggestion: after dying 'she is no witch *anymore*'. However, by arguing not to believe in witches as witches can die, J and L construct a witch being which lives, or exists, at least until it dies. From a western perspective this way of arguing is paradoxical as J and L show to 'believe' in the existence of witches by the way they explain that they *don't* 'believe' in witches.

When, in line 31, the interviewer confronts J and L with what she logically inferred from the respondent's assertions -that some people *are* witches before they die- J and L circumvent to answer. L laughs (line 32) and repeats that she does not, and moreover *can*not believe in witches (line 35). The respondents give some other explanations for their disbelief, which are from a western perspective paradoxical as well. They make clear that they have '*never* seen' witches (line 35) and you 'can't, you don't *know*' that that person is a witch' (line 43). Hereby J suggests that somebody could in principle be a witch, although perceiving somebody's witch-nature is impossible. Again, by explaining why they do not believe in witches, J and L construct their 'belief' in the reality of witches, something that they explicitly and straightforwardly stated in the beginning of the interview.

A western observer is likely to find it difficult to reconcile the claim of existence and the claim of disbelief. Nevertheless, the women don't attend to any contradictions in their claims. Apparently Christian Malawians can justifiably assert that they don't 'believe' in something, of which they can say at the same time that it does exist. In the next paragraph this issue of the meaning of 'believing' in Malawian Christians' discourse will be tackled.

6.2 Claims of belief and claims of reality: Of a different order

For western observers the extracts discussed in the previous paragraph contained some ambiguities, contradictions and paradoxes. Extract 16 is paradoxical in that J and L claim that there are witches, and at the same time they assert not to believe in them. When the interviewer probes after their ideas about the existence of witches, they give ambiguous, circumventing answers. The respondents themselves did not attend spontaneously to their 'illogical' reasonings about witches or ancestral spirits. Extract 17 strikes as contradictory because the respondent distances himself from ancestral spirits and debunks a rain calling-ritual, which is directed at these spirits, but he does claim elsewhere in the interview that ancestral spirits exist. As said in the outline of the analytic perspective in chapter 2, individuals produce meaning in their verbal and non-verbal interactions. Using phrases like 'believing in' implies that different meanings will emerge, and that might explain why Malawian Christians' reasoning about their belief in and the reality of witches or ancestral spirits sometimes strikes a western observer, but not a Malawian Christian, as contradictory and paradoxical. Hence, in the following extracts I will examine the meanings of 'believing in' as produced locally, in concrete discursive actions.

Extract 18 R7

1. I   But you wouldn't say that as a Christian you shouldn't believe in those.
2. R   Yes, you shouldn't believe in it.
3. I   But, but, but, they are there?
4. R   There are there!, I am sure, they are there. And they come to you through this type of coming. With
5. somebody who starts shouting or doing this and that.
6. I   But then I was wondering, I don't know, could you explain me because you say you shouldn't believe
7. in them, but they are there (.). But if you say they are there isn't that kind of the same as believing in
8. them, or (.), or what's the difference?
9. R   Ehm (2). Jesus Christ at one time had come across a mad person who shouted at Jesus and asked for a
10. herb and he drove bad spirits from this man and bad spirits entered into it. It means even Jesus knew
11. there were bad spirits. And the bad spirits knew Jesus. These are the sort of say spirits, which we are
12. not to believe. They can (count on you?) and you can cast hem to hell.
13. I   hmhm, ja I see.
14. R   So they are there. You have heard them talking in this way. You have heard people at least dreaming
15. thing (true question have) there are always people have talked about it. Actually they come in person
16. in a dream and tell them I want you to do this, to brew beer so so and so.

17. (…)
18. (both laugh)

In line 2 the respondent immediately and straightforwardly confirms the interviewer's suggestion that as a Christian you should not believe in ancestral spirits. When asked about the existence of ancestral spirits (line 4) the respondent states that ancestral spirits 'are there'. By repeating this claim, using a stressing intonation, and his assertion 'I am sure' (line 4), he pleads for the existence of ancestral spirits in a convinced way. In lines 4-5 and 14-16 the respondent engages in 'empiricist accounting' (Edwards & Potter, 1992). He argues, referring to spirit possession, that one can observe that ancestral spirits come to people when they start shouting 'or doing this and that' (line 5). In line 15 the respondent refers to dreams in which spirits 'actually' come in person. In lines 14 and 15 the respondent generalises his observances, making his 'empiricist accounting' more generally valid. He does this by speaking in general terms '*you* have heard' (line 14) instead of using a personal form '*I* have heard'. In line 15 he says, 'always people have talked about it'.

The respondent's claim that there are certain ancestral spirits is difficult to reconcile with his statement that 'you shouldn't believe in it' (line 2). In lines 6 and 7 the interviewer asks the respondent to explain the difference between 'believing in' ancestral spirits and saying 'they are there'. After a short pause he initiates a 'repair' in line 8: he refers to a biblical story in which ancestral spirits are mentioned. Thereby he shows himself to be someone who reads and knows the bible. Moreover, he makes clear that also Christianity acknowledges the existence of ancestral spirits: 'even Jesus knew there were bad spirits.' and moreover, 'the bad spirits knew Jesus.' (Line 11). Here, the respondent constructs claiming that there are spirits as *not* unchristian and prevents being judged himself as 'unchristian' because of his claim that ancestral spirits 'are there'. The respondent constructs a taken for granted reality of ancestral spirits, which is omnipresent and thus also valid for Christians. Before extract 14 the respondent asserted 'I don't believe in the ancestral spirit. But this happens. We just see it …'. He constructs the ATR-reality not only as taken for granted and omnipresent but also as coercive. Ancestral spirits can just come to you, if you are Christian. The respondent uses the discursive device called before 'externalisation' to unproblematise his claims about the reality of ancestral spirits. The coercive, omnipresent reality of ATR makes it self-evident and inevitable that people claim there are ancestral spirits. However, it does not forestall that one should not and does not have to believe in ancestral spirits: 'these are the sort of say spirits which we are not to believe and you cast them to hell' (line 12).

Apparently, Malawian Christians can use 'believing in' x in a way which makes it not identical to claiming existence of x. More specifically, 'not believing in' does not mean not acknowledging existence: Malawian Christians can claim not to believe and still make ontologic claims about ATR-entities like witches and ancestral spirits.

Investigating language-in-use in the next extracts will make clear not only what believing in does not, but what it *can* mean in Christian Malawians' talk.

Extract 19 R2 1/17

1. I   But in Malawi when people, I think, are Christian and I think that many people, they do for example
2.   believe in ancestral spirits.
3. R   Not really…
4. I   Not really..
5. R   Yes
6. I   they don't?
7. R   They don't believe in these ancestral spirits, yes. Because most Christian are not doing what what
8.   these ancestral spirits can ask people to do. Yes.
9.   (some lines omitted)
10. I But for example if someone ehm, becomes possessed by an ancestral spirit in a certain way, if an
11.   ancestral spirit comes into someone that happens sometimes.
12. R That happens.
13. I But, does it also happen to Christians?
14. R Yes, that will happen even to Christians, yes.
15. I So then, if it happens to a Christian, then such a person does believe in a Christian God and in
16.   ancestral spirits doesn't he?
17. R No, he believes only in the Christian God. But these spirits have just come to attempt whether he or
18.   She can believe in this ancestral spirits so that this can change the behaviour of this man to do evil things
19. Yes.

In line 3, the respondent asserts that people in Malawi do 'not really' believe in ancestral spirits. Although this strikes a westerner as ambiguous and vague, the respondent does not orient to a need for clarification. Only after probing of the interviewer in line 6, he explains that people don't believe in ancestral spirits, as they do not do what ancestral spirits ask them to do (line 7). Hereby he attends to the reality of spirits by taking into account the existence of spirits, which can ask people to do something. In line 12-14 he states that people, even Christians, become possessed. By saying with a neutral intonation 'that happens', he constructs spirit possession as a self-evident event which is at least not very rare. Again, from a western perspective, a contradiction emerges: the respondent says that people don't believe in ancestral spirits. At the same time, he claims that people become possessed. From a western perspective one would conclude that if people assert that they or others become possessed, they show that they themselves or others believe in ancestral spirits. In this extract the respondent himself does not attend to any ambiguity or contradiction; he does not spontaneously give any clarification. Moreover, when the interviewer confronts him in lines 17 and 18 with the contradiction she perceives, the respondent holds on to his claim; 'he only believe in the Christian God. But the spirits do attempt whether he or she can believe so that this can change the behaviour.' Like the respondent in extract 15, the respondent here engages in 'externalisation' when the interviewer presses him to make his claim intelligible for her. In lines 17 and 18 he warrants his claim that someone who only believes in God can become possessed, by putting the cause of this spirit possession outside individuals themselves. A Christian can't be blamed if a spirit comes to him and seduces him or her to 'believe' in this spirit. Again we can see that the respondent uses 'believing in' in such a way that its meaning is not identical to an ontological claim about the reality of spirits. Rather, 'believing in' is used in such a way that it obtains a meaning of acting in accordance with the wishes of, in this case, ancestral spirits.

The next extract shows as well that claiming to belief in the working of ATR-practices or the existence of ATR-entities is problematic, rather than claiming the reality of phenomena like witchcraft. Before extract 19, the respondent has told the interviewer that he consulted a witchdoctor once, who told him he was bewitched and gave him herbs.

Extract 19a R2 1/17

1. I   And that herbs which can help you that you are protected against witchcraft?
2. R   Partly I can say that, yes...
3. I   Partly
4. R   Partly.
5. I   And the other part, haha?
6. R   The other partly because I am a Christian believer so I dont exactly believe that these witchcraft are
7.   being healed by the what, they are being protected by these traditional healer, yeah.

When the respondent is asked whether the herbs protected him against witchcraft he says 'partly I can say that' (line 2). Again we see an ambiguous answer, which is not spontaneously elucidated. Only when the interviewer probes a second time (line 5) the respondent gives some clarification. He points out that as he is a Christian believer he does not 'exactly believe' that traditional healers protect against witchcraft (line 6). What J shows to be problematic for Christians is to 'believe' that traditional healers, or traditional herbs, can protect against witchcraft. Note that he does not problematise the 'belief' in witchcraft itself. Indeed, later on in the interview the respondent makes clear that he did think there was witchcraft in his environment when he was ill.

Regularly respondents stress that one should not believe in witches, ancestral spirits or traditional healers as God is the one who is almighty and powerful. It has been mentioned before that respondents can construct Christianity as superior to ATR, thereby downgrading and debunking ATR. It becomes clear now how Malawian Christians can use 'Christian Superiority' also to unproblematise ATR and to acknowledge an ATR-reality. Ancestral spirits or witches *real*, they are only not as mighty as the Christian God. It seems to be unproblematic to 'confess' as Malawian Christian that supernatural forces and entities, which belong to ATR, are real, provided that Christianity is granted enough –read more than ATR- power and importance. Thus one can claim the reality of ATR 'entities' but one should not 'believe' in it. Malawian Christians use 'believe in' in their talk in such a way that as long as one shows not to direct ones behaviour at ancestral spirits or witches, or at least not out of free will, one does not 'believe in' the ATR-reality.

6.3 Christian and ATR-practices: Of a different order

In the previous section I have shown that reality claims and claims of disbelief cannot be equated; they are two things of a different kind. Also the next extracts show that Christianity and ATR are attended to and constructed as two things of a different kind. This makes salient, as did the investigation of the way phrases like 'believing in' versus 'they are there' or 'they exist' are used by Christian Malawians, that western researchers should be wary of imposing an artificial order from above on local phenomena.

Extract 20 is a passage from an interview with one of the informants, a reverend. He makes clear how one should deal with the ATR-reality as Christian.

Extract 20

1. I   But then, what if for example people of your parish… if it is said that a certain man or woman that
2.   he is bewitched and he is suffering…
3. R   And the issue is brought before the church?
4. I   Hmhm
5. R   Yeah what it is, I have been involved in some other cases concerning magic. Some other people
6.   brought to our attention such such and such a person has done this to us. We told them no, the church
7.   has no mandate to at least advice on this one. This is outside the church. Go home and handle this at
8.   your own place with you village-headman and some other elders in your society. The church has
9.   nothing to do with witchcraft.
10. I   Ja ja, ja ja so then in a way you say okay, we as a church we can't help you, maybe you are bewitched
11.   1but we.[can't do anything
12. R   [we can't do anything on that one because it is not our jurisdiction. We bring people to Christ
13.   we are not bringing people to. I mean to get perished. We are preaching the good news so that people,

14. everybody should live her own way of living and emulate and take Christ's what way of living. You
15. see.
16. I   But you would advice then such a person for example to go to their home villages, and perhaps there
17. might be someone called who can help them, or.
18. R   Of course they do go somewhere and they meet possibly somebody who can at least come up with
19. (help?) I mean that's none of our business as a church. As a church we have nothing to do with that
20. yeah.
21. (interviewer tells she understood that the CCAP doesn't acknowledge the existence of witchcraft.)
22. I think to rule out saying that the CCAP's church in Malawi is ruling out of witchcraft, that is wrong.
23. That is not true. Because we live in this society where we know that witchcraft is existing. And you
24. can't stand in church saying there's no witchcraft. That is not true. Witchcraft is there, it was there it
25. is there, ever it will be there. But what we do we civic-educate our Christians. To rely in Christ. To
26. depend on Jesus as their saviour. That's our direction. Not by saying there' s no witchcraft there is
27. nothing, no it is for ever to be there. But people should at least look at Jesus as their sustainer. And
28. (prefector..?) of their hope as Christians. Yeah.

In extract 20 the reverend acknowledges the existence of witchcraft without reservation (lines 22-28). He generalises this ontological claim to 'the CCAP church in Malawi', for 'you can't stand in church saying there's no witchcraft.' (line 24). In so doing, he makes this ontological claim extra convincing and unproblematises making such a claim as a Christian. For, if the whole church acknowledges the existence of witchcraft, it must not be problematic. Moreover, the reverend makes clear that even if you are a Christian you can, or even have to, acknowledge witchcraft. However, the reverend does strictly separate the taking of concrete actions, which are directed at this ATR-'belief' from Christianity. He points out that people who have problems related to witchcraft should be referred to the village-headman and elderly people in the home-village. The Christian church does not and cannot advice in witchcraft-matters: 'The church has no mandate to at least advice on this one. This is outside the church.... The church has nothing to do with witchcraft' (line 6). The only thing the church can do is to 'civic-educate our Christians. To rely in Christ. To depend on Jesus as their saviour' (line 22). Again, it can be observed how the superiority of Christianity is constructed and that by implication this unproblematises the ATR-'belief' in witchcraft. One can claim that there is witchcraft, as long as one makes clear to rely on Christ and to depend on Him as Saviour. The reverend shows to work on a Christian identity-project and to stimulate others to work on their Christian identity-project as well.

This reverend constructs Christianity and ATR as two things of a different kind, belonging to two different domains of action. The reality of ATR permeates in the domain of Christianity, but in this Christian domain one cannot deal with this reality. Therefore one has to go figuratively and literally outside the church.

In the following three extracts the respondents talk about Christian practices. These extracts demonstrate, in a different way, that Christian Malawians attend to and construct Christianity and African Traditional Religion as belonging to a different order.

Extract 21 R13 1/18

1. I Ehm. Ehm when you were ill ehm all the different times during your life, ehm do you also happen to
2. ask God for help or something or?
3. R That's the most thing, the most important thing which I I normally do. I and my family, after supper 4. we have to pray to God. To thank him as for what he has done for us that day. Now in the morning,
5. we included as well in .the prayer, in our daily prayer.

Extract 22 R8 4/10

1. I Hmhm, and about the Christian-initaion rite, would you like them to go to a Christian
2. initiation rite?
3. R Yes, I think I would love that very much. Because that one they would benefit from both ends whereby

4. their spiritual life would be guided and also their social life. The way they are supposed to live and
5. grow in society (.) They would be taught how to live (.) So I would really love them to go to such and
6. initiation.

Extract 23 R9 2/8

1. I (…), would you like certain traditional elements to be in your own funeral, or would you definitely
2. not like that or doesn't it matter or
3. R Eh I would not like that to happen at my funeral. I I , because I am a Christian I can not have them at
4. my funeral because it would be the church-ritual, who take that in my funeral rather then those other
5. things. Because the people they fear the Nyau, (tells about people running away because of Nyau) so I
6. would not love to have a funeral of that kind. I would just like people, Christian (friends?) to come
7. and maybe they sing () usually they conduct some prayers and they go singing to the graveyard, I
8. would love that to have that at my funeral rather then ()

In extract 21 the respondent asserts that asking God for help is 'the most important thing' which he 'normally' does (line 3). By pointing at the regularity of his prayers – he speaks about 'normally' and makes clear he prays twice a day- and by using the superlative in '*most* important' (line 3), the respondent shows how highly he values praying to God. Also in extract 22 strong words are used to express appreciation for a Christian practice: 'I would really *love* them [his children] to go to such an initiation.' (Line 4). In extract 23, the respondent rejects a traditional Nyau funeral, which he contrasts with a Christian funeral. Also this respondent expresses 'love' (line 7) for this Christian practice.

However, although these respondents stress their involvement in Christianity, they do not completely discard traditional religious practices. The respondent of extract 21 for whom praying to God is 'the most important thing', did elaborately explain in preceding passages when and why he has consulted a traditional healer. He also claims that he will consult one in the future 'dependent on the disease'. When the respondent in extract 22 is asked just before whether he regrets that his ethnic group, the Tonga, doesn't have initiations, he replies 'to some extent I would say it is' and points out the usefulness of initiations. The respondent of extract 23 rejects the Nyau Traditional Funeral, writ large, but later he straightforwardly asserts that he performed some specific traditional funeral rites, like washing of the hair with traditional medicines after the burial and sweeping around the grave. Thus, extracts 21, 22 and 23 show that Malawian Christians can attribute much importance to Christianity, without having to choose for Christianity *instead of* for ATR. ATR and Christianity are not necessarily mutual exclusive categories.

Notice that the respondents in extract 21 and 22 put forward their high appreciation for Christianity after the interviewer asked them about the meaning of Christianity in their lives. This suggests as well that comparing and contrasting ATR- with Christian-practices is not a necessary and not always a self-evident thing to do for Malawian Christians. This appeared as well when the accounts Debunking and Perceived Risk were discussed. Christian Malawians who used these accounts appeared to reject ATR more for pragmatic than ideological reasons. They engaged in practical talk, in which they did not make relevant Christianity. It becomes clear that one should be careful to presume that Malawian Christians consider Christian practices as 'counterparts' of ATR-practices. Like Fabian (1985) said, observers of religious practices should be careful not to seek for too much logical coherence and should not impose artificial order from above.

The respondents who featured in extracts 21 to 23 grant relevance to both ATR and Christian-practices, but make their appreciation for the latter much more explicit. Respondents frequently express high appreciation for Christianity, especially by using superlatives. Malawian Christians do show that ATR-practices are relevant as well, but don't stress their appreciation for these practices. For example, respondents never say that they 'love' ATR-practices, an expression which they frequently use for Christian practices. It seems to be more appropriate to be explicit about ones value of Christian practices than traditional practices. In addition, claims about one's involvement in Christianity are often used for a Christian identity-project. Claims about one's involvement in ATR on the other hand appear to function less as identity-claims; when talking about ATR respondents tend to engage in practical rather than ideological talk. This again suggests that Malawian Christians attend to and therefore construct traditional religious practices and beliefs and Christianity in a different way, as things of a different kind. This can be observed in extract 24, displayed below. This extract shows how respondents can sanction the conversation-partners who erroneously cast ATR-practices and Christianity in the same categories.

Extract 24 R13 2/2

(Interviewer tells she heard about certain birth rituals in Malawi and asks whether he performed birth-rituals on some of his eight children)

1. R Ehm of course that has happened to my children yes. Eh as I told you earlier, we have to, I respect the
2. traditional culture.
3. (respondent tells that the bath had to protect the head and the whole body, for which he related to the idea 'what the eh old .people say' that when a man is a polygamist a child should be protected from whatever he does'. Hereby M. refers to the idea that when fathers of just born babies commit adultery they endanger the well-being of the child.)
3. I Ehm and were your children also baptised?
4. R Ehm the first four children were baptised after they have grown up. But the other four were baptised
5. soon after they are born. A few months after their birth.
6. Ehm now I was wondering, ehm I can imagine that, probably not my own opinion, but what if
7. someone, but imagine that someone would say eh ask you, isn't that the same thing in a way to baptise
8. a child and to perform
9. No, no, no, no. They are different things all together
10. Aha they are not similar things. Okay
11. I No. They are very different. (some lines omitted)
12. R But that does not concern whatever he has been bathing does not concern the church because that
13. your own, you may baptise him, you may not baptise him. Sorry, you may bath him, you may not
14. bath him, but it is up to the family. If the family wants, it's up to them. But the church does not ehm
15. encourage people to do that
16. [ ]
17. I And if you say that the church doesn't encourage the bathing and all that, ehm do they also discourage

18. it or do they don't ?
19. R   No eh not specifically, the church does not discourage the bath, but what the church discourages is the
20. practising of witchcraft. And eh all sorts of things which are evil. But they don't specifically say that
21. bathing a child is a wrong thing, no, no.

From a western perspective, one might be inclined to compare birth rituals with baptism. Indeed one of the advocates of the Roman Catholic policy of inculturation, Father Boucher designed a ritual in which he combined elements of birth rituals with elements of Christian baptism. However, when the interviewer suggested to the respondent that birth rituals are similar to baptism (lines 11-13), he strongly corrected her (line 15). The respondent makes clear that they are 'very different' (lines 15,17) and that birth rituals do not belong to the concerns of the church (lines 19). He makes the correction emphatic by repeating 'no' four times (line 15) and 'very' twice (line 17), and by adding that baptism and birth rituals are different things 'all together' (line 15). Moreover, in lines 26 and 27 the respondent makes clear that the church does not condemn birth rituals and that this ATR-practice does not belong to 'all sorts of things which are evil' like witchcraft. Thus M constructs baptism and birth rituals as two things of a different kind, and the performing of birth rituals as *not* unchristian.

The respondent in extract 24 does not disinterestedly correct a wrong perception. The biting reaction in lines 15 and 17 suggests that there's something at stake: the respondent seems to anticipate a possible counterclaim that he is not a devoted Christian. He makes clear that birth rituals have nothing to do with Christianity and in lines 26 to 28 he points out that they don't belong to the 'evil' things, which the church discourages. Hereby he constructs himself as a Christian who performs birth rituals but did not break any church rules and did not do anything amoral.

It becomes clear that whereas western people are inclined to compare and equate ATR-practices with certain Christian practices, Malawian Christians frequently relate to them as two things of a different order. If a western person shows to a Malawian Christian to equate ATR-practices and beliefs with certain Christian –practices and beliefs, Malawian Christians will put effort to correct this perspective. They have to, for if their ATR-involvement would be of the same order as their Christianity, they would abide two masters. This is something, which is, for Malawians who are sincere Christians, not done; it would make them 'syncretists' in the old pejorative sense of the word.

Intermezzo IV

Now insight has been gained in Malawian Christians' ambivalent accounting practices, let us see whether we can understand now the 'logic' of the ambiguous, contradictory extract, which has been portrayed before in Intermezzo I.

Extract 25 R2 2/2

1. I   But do you also think then that Malawians who are also Christians, that they shouldn't go to
2. R   traditional healers actually?
3. I   I think that is better, because when most of the Malawians can go to the traditional healer I think that
4. will make them not to believe in God. Yes.
5. I   Ja Ja But it doesn't, it can't go together, that you for example that you and go to the traditional healer
6. and that you believe in God?
7. R   Ah no, it cant go together.
8. I   And, but, because I am wondering because I think you told me yesterday that you consulted some
9. traditional healers sometimes..
10. R   Yes
11. I   Ehm but you are also Christian..
12. R   Yah.
13. I   How do you, haha, see that then?
14. R   Oh, on my part I do this because ah I do believe God. Not that I believe on his traditional healers, yah
15. only what I do is that, I do it because of some what, something which might happen at home is what
16. made me to go to the traditional healers. But not that I believe of them, yes.
17. I   But something that happened at home, what do you mean by that exactly?
18. R   I mean according to how we are staying there at home as we are now, we are only now children. We

19.	have a grandmother who is what, not in the position to handle things, or even to.. She can't cook she
20.	can't go to fetch water she can't do nothing we are only now children who are looking one after another.
21.	So due to the death of our what our parents, yah.
22.	I Hm Hm and therefore you felt that it was kind of necessary to go to traditional healers sometimes...
23.	R Yes it's necessary to go there after you face some troubles. Because if it is what,
24.	I the witchcraft are doing these things then the traditional healer can assist you to prevent this witchcraft.
25.	R Yah yah so then you think that actually Christians shouldn't go to traditional healers but there might
26.	be certain circumstances that there are problems in your life, and then you have to go there, or...
27.	I No I am not saying that all Christians should go the traditional healers due to certain circumstances
28.	which they are facing. Because I am saying on my side I don't know whether some of the Christians
29.	can do that because most of the Christians in the CCAP believe that Jesus is the one who can heal
30.	everything. So I do that only because of what, because of how things are going on at home, yes.

In lines 2 to 3 and 7, the respondent makes clear that consulting traditional healers and believing in God 'can not go together'. This is remarkable as this Christian respondent asserted before that he consulted traditional healers himself. When the interviewer tries to confront him with this contradiction assertion (lines 8 and 9) he does not give any 'repair'-account. He merely expresses 'Yah' (line 12) as reply to the interviewers remark 'but you are also Christian' (line 11), and does thus not attend to anything incompatible about his being Christian and his consulting of traditional healers. Nor does the respondent attend to anything contradictory about his claims that 'the two can not go together' and that he consulted traditional healers himself. Thus, the respondent does what we have seen more often; he attends to Christianity and traditional healing as two of a different kind, not interfering with each other.

Only when, in line 14, he is directly asked to elucidate his claims, he stresses that he does believe in God and that he does not believe in traditional healers. Repeating this claim in line 16, aids the respondent's positioning as someone who does not believe in traditional healers. He 'only' (line 14) consulted traditional healers due to something what 'might happen at home' (line 16). The discursive device, which the respondent uses here, is what has been called before 'Situational Coercion'. By using words like 'only' (line 14) and his utterance 'Oh' (line 14), he trivialises his ATR-involvement. In the same line the respondent stresses that it was he himself who consulted traditional healers by saying 'on *my* part, *I* do this'. This contrasts with the general terms in which he phrases his declaration of incompatibility: 'when *most* of *the Malawians*' (line 3). The interviewer provides an upshot of what the respondent has said in lines 25-26. Hereby she fixates and generalises his statement about his particular action in a particular situation, especially by using phrases like 'certain circumstance*s*' and 'problem*s* in your life' –note the plural forms- that make that 'you have to go there'. In line 27 the respondent disagrees with the interviewer's upshot. The respondent makes relevant the specific nature of his claim by stressing that it was only in this specific situation that he could justifiably consult traditional healers - 'on my side I don't know' (line 28) and 'So I do that only' (line 30)- and that he does not unproblematise this in general or on principle: 'No I am not saying that all Christians should go...' (Line 27).

It can be concluded that the respondent constructs on principle consulting traditional healers and believing in God as on principle incompatible. At the same time, he is also capable of making his consulting of traditional healers justified by using a mixture of the externalisation accounts 'Situational Coercion' and 'Risk Reducing'. In so doing, he makes clear that he was forced to deal with the ATR-practice. J makes clear that he does not deal with ATR on the same level as he deals with Christianity; he does not structurally attend to ATR, and not with the same kind of commitment as he has for Christianity. He 'believes' in God, not in the traditional healer. Judging from the way the respondent uses 'believe' in his accounts, it obtains again a meaning of structurally, intrinsically motivated 'attending to'. Like other respondents, he makes clear that you don't 'believe' in ATR-entities –in this case traditional healers- if you can show that you only occasionally, because you are forced, take them into account and therefore turn to ATR-practices. In their claims about 'believing' and 'not believing', Malawian Christians show an ideological commitment to Christianity and a predominantly pragmatic orientation to ATR. Thereby they accomplish that ATR-involvement does not endanger their Christian identity-project.

Note that in extract 25 it is demonstrated again that the ATR-reality is unproblematic for Malawian Christians. When the respondent problematises the consulting of traditional healers on Christian grounds, he does not make relevant anything problematic about 'believing' in the existence of witches as Christian. On the contrary, the respondent makes relevant witches and witchcraft –that are so real that he had to seek protection for them- to justify his own consulting of witchdoctors. But this reality of ATR is of a different order than the Christian faith.

Conclusion

As we have seen before, Malawian Christians construct a particular version of reality in which witches and ancestral spirits are self-evident and irrefutably real. Often, Malawian Christians do not construct these claims about the reality of ATR as interfering with their Christian commitment. However, at the same time Malawian Christians do make clear that they don't believe in the ATR-entities. It has become clear that they use 'believing in' in talk about ATR in such a way that it obtains different meanings than the one western people are used to. Their reality claims cannot be equated with claiming to 'believe in' ancestral spirits or witches. Claiming existence of supernatural ATR-entities like witches and ancestral spirits is taken for granted, inevitable and thus justified, claiming to believe in them is not. 'Believing in' a supernatural entity is used in such a way that it obtains a meaning like structurally, purposefully and intrinsically motivated 'attending to' this entity. Warranted 'believing in' appears to be something which is restricted to the Christian God and which is kept outside the domain of the ATR-reality. Malawian Christians refer in their talk to witches and ancestral spirits and to their Christian faith in such a way that they construct the two as belonging to a different order. Thus, Malawian Christians who acknowledge the reality of ATR can still claim that ATR and Christianity cannot go together. For, as Malawian Christians refer to the reality of ATR as belonging to a different order, a different world, than their Christian faith, they show that ATR and Christianity are not going together. When pressed to account for their claims of existence of ancestral spirits and witches, respondents give different unproblematising accounts whereby they place the two at a different level and show not to abide two masters.

7. Conclusion and Discussion

7.1 Conclusion

In this qualitative, cultural psychological research Malawian Christians' talk about ATR-involvement has been studied.

Malawian Christians assert to perform several practices and to have various beliefs, which can be said to belong to their African traditional religion. At the same time, they strike as devoted members of a church –public displays of church membership are abundant in Malawi- which, on the whole, disapproves of Christians' ATR-involvement. This raised the question of how the Malawian Christians manage to be both devoted Christians and to be involved in ATR.

Using discourse analysis, interview-extracts have been studied into detail, in order to gain insight into the way Malawian Christians account for their own or others involvement in ATR. Do they problematise it or not, and especially, how do the respondents accomplish (un)problematisation? Furthermore, what else can Malawian Christian respondents achieve by describing and accounting for ATR-involvement in the way they do?

Malawian Christians appear to give several accounts in which they problematise ATR practices and –beliefs. Sometimes the problematising leads to a straightforward rejection of ATR on grounds of Christianity. But not always do Christian Malawians who reject ATR construct ATR and Christianity as mutual exclusive categories. Christian Malawians can problematise ATR without making relevant Christianity or their Christian identity. Sometimes accounting Malawian Christians put effort to position themselves as modern, western people instead of showing to be devoted Christians. And frequently respondents do not show to work on an 'identity-project' at all; they reject ATR for pragmatic reasons. For example, they reject ATR-practices because they do not work or are harmful for one's well-being.

However, further investigation of discourse about ATR showed that the Malawian Christian respondents also account in such a way for own or fellow Christians' ATR-involvement that they 'unproblematise' this involvement. Again, different accounts have been identified by which they justify ATR-involvement by externalising, normalising and trivialising it. When externalising the interviewed Christian Malawians make clear that they can find themselves in a situation in their daily life in which they are forced to deal with ATR, whether they are Christians or not. When normalising, they convince their conversation-partner that it is logical and normal to deal with ATR. When trivialising they make clear that their ATR-involvement was incidental, for superficial reasons. Overall, they position themselves as persons who perform certain practices or have certain 'beliefs', but do not structurally, or out of an 'intrinsic motivation', attend to ATR. Hereby they safeguard their ideological commitment to Christianity, which demands that on principle one should not deal with ATR as Christian.

Although investigation of the unproblematising accounts make us understand how Christians can discursively manage to justify ATR-involvement, it does not provide sufficient insight into the (re-) production of the contradictory, ambivalent accounting-pattern. Several contradictions and ambiguities emerged. First, the Malawian Christians *both* problematise *and* unproblematise ATR, in combination with instances in which ATR-practices or beliefs were simply not accounted for and thus neither problematised nor unproblematised. Second, respondents claimed the reality and existence of ATR-entities like witches and spirits but stated at the same time not to believe in them.

In order to come to an understanding of these ambiguities and contradictions, one should not look for a specific psychological make-up, but investigate interactional mechanisms, which generate the discerned pattern of accounting. Broadly speaking, three issues can be identified which should be taken into account, or looked into, in order to understand the contradictions and ambivalences in Malawian Christians' talk about ATR. The first, basic, issue which should be taken into account in order to understand the contradictions and ambiguities, is that meanings are produced in language-in-use, which is always situated in local contexts (cf. Baerveldt, 1999, cf. Wittgenstein, 1953). Therefore, it should not be assumed that western ways of attributing meaning and making sense are equivalent to Christian Malawians' ways of making sense. Second, in order to gain insight in to the way Malawian Christian respondents can both problematise, unproblematise ATR involvement and treat it as not accountable, it should be acknowledged that, like interaction partners always do, Christian Malawians will orient to a judging interviewer and wider audience while talking about ATR. Related to this is a third issue: one needs to look at the different kinds of talk in which the respondents appear to engage, which are at least partly afforded by the western interviewer. In what follows I will elaborate on these three issues.

The local production of meaning, which forestalls that one can sensibly make sense of phenomena from one's own western analytic perspective, becomes clear when one investigates the apparent contradictions in Christian Malawians claims of the reality of, but disbelief in, ATR-entities. When unproblematising, but also when problematising involvement in ATR, accounting Christian Malawians attend to and construct a taken for granted, omnipresent ATR-reality. Malawian Christians regularly claim in a self-evidential, casual way that ATR-entities like ancestral spirits and witches are real. At the same time Malawian Christians make clear that they do not to believe in ATR-entities. Although from a western perspective this strikes as contradictory, scrutinizing local discursive interactions make clear that one has to be careful using one's own assumptions or framework to gain insight in phenomena. Unlike westerners, Malawian Christians don't equate 'believing in' with claiming existence. Malawian Christians use 'believing in' in such a way that it obtains meanings like structurally, purposefully directing once actions at something. Thereby 'believing in' belongs to Christianity to which they are ideologically committed, not to the domain of the ATR-reality.

In addition, although from a western perspective one may be inclined to equate or compare ATR and Christianity as two things of the same kind – namely religion-, such an assumption does not do justice to the way Malawian Christians orient to Christianity and ATR. They usually attend to and construct the ATR-reality and accompanying practices as of a different order than their Christian faith. From a western perspective one might consider certain Christian practices as equivalent to certain ATR-practices, like Christian and traditional initiation rites or baptism and birth rites. However, often Malawian Christians do not attend to them as being each other's counterparts. Frequently they appear not to perceive ATR and Christianity as oppositional categories between which they should choose. Thus, Malawian Christians can acknowledge the ATR-reality, deal with its practices *and* make a principle, ideological statement that ATR and Christianity cannot go together. Malawian Christians' ATR-involvement is not going together with their Christianity as they -literally and figuratively- keep ATR outside the church.

The fact that Malawian Christians do not always attend to the ATR-reality in an unproblematic way, seems to be related to their orienting to 'others'

– especially the western researcher - as affording certain actions and certain ways of accounting (Shotter, 1989). Malawian Christians have to take care that they attend to ATR in a way, which is justified for devoted Christians, who are members of a church, which on principle claims a religious monopoly. They have to meet the social demand of not serving to masters of the same kind. When the western researcher presses Malawian Christians to account for their ATR-involvement, she suggests to them that she perceives or might perceive Christianity and ATR as two of the same kind. Anticipating to the claim of a 'judging audience' that they are insincere, 'syncretistic' Christians, Malawian Christians give different accounts whereby they problematise ATR-involvement or unproblematise certain forms. Tuning their verbal actions to the interviewer's, they construct their ATR practices and beliefs at a different level than Christianity. They show that they highly value Christianity and that they are committed to the Christian church. On principle they follow the church-rules, but in certain situations they might deal with ATR. However, unlike their involvement in Christianity, their ATR-involvement is not structural, and they are not intrinsically motivated for it. Christian Malawians attend to and construct the ATR-reality as omnipresent and coercive, which makes it hardly possible to step outside this particular version of reality. Malawian Christians construct witches and ancestral spirits as supernatural entities that impinge themselves upon people, whether you are Christian or not. However, they don't 'believe in' these entities, they 'believe in' God. All throughout, God remains the superior, almighty sovereign.

Furthermore, as said, looking into the different kinds of talk respondents engage can provide insight into the ambivalence of Malawian Christians who both problematise, unproblematise ATR *and* sometimes do not treat it as accountable at all. Analysis of Malawian Christians' discourse about ATR has made clear that Malawian Christians can engage in different kinds of talk when talking to a western researcher. Following Slugoski and Ginsburg (in Shotter & Gergen, 1989) one kind of talk has been called 'identity talk'. This is a rhetorical, ideological kind of discourse in which Christian Malawians position themselves either as critical, educated, modern individuals or as devoted Christians. Often these identity-positions go together. When carrying out a modern identity-project they show to reject ATR-practices and –beliefs because they know that they are useless, nonsensical or even harmful. Hereby they forestall to be judged as primitive or backward. When carrying out a Christian identity-project, they show to be devoted Christians who, out of commitment to Christianity, reject ATR. Hereby ATR and Christianity are frequently constructed as incompatible, oppositional categories. They construct them as two religions, of the same order, which 'can not go together' and should not be mixed. The accounts, which are especially, used for this Christian 'identity talk' are 'Legislative Rejection' and 'Christian Moralising'.

It is often the interviewer who invites Malawian Christians respondents to partake in this ideological discourse by virtue of her questions. For example, when she asks respondents to reflect on the church-policy with regard to ATR, the interviewer affords the respondents to engage in a Christian identity-project. As we have seen they readily accept this invitation, for example by showing to highly value Christianity and its Christian practices.

Besides 'identity talk', Christian Malawians also engage in less rhetorical and more 'practical' talk, in which they reject certain ATR-practices and – beliefs for rather pragmatic reasons. The Malawian Christian respondents partake in this kind of practical discourse for example when giving accounts like 'Debunking', 'Perceived Risk', 'Risk Reducing' or 'Obeying Others'.

Especially in this pragmatic talk, which pertains concrete situations and problems in life, Malawian Christians can accept and condone ATR-practices and beliefs. Not the religious character but the practical, functional aspects of ATR-practices are made relevant. It is especially in this kind of practical discourse ATR and Christianity belong to a different order; one is a worthy Religion, the other a collection of 'mundane' ideas about reality and useful practices. Hence, in this kind of practical discourse engaging in ATR as a Christian is not treated as accountable and constructed as unproblematic.

When respondents talk about ATR-practices, they frequently switch between ideological identity-talk and practical discourse. If they give pragmatic arguments to reject ATR, they will often also use arguments, which make relevant their Christian membership as well.

We have come to an understanding of the ambivalent and contradictory accounting-pattern that Christians both reject ATR, claim to be involved in ATR and condone this involvement. In an ideological discourse Malawian Christians will predominantly reject ATR. Thereby they show to be committed to Christianity and its rules, or to be modern Malawians. In a more practical discourse they can straightforwardly acknowledge the ATR-reality and assert to perform ATR-practices, without necessarily accounting for it. ATR is not attended to as a religion like Christianity; the two are of a different kind. When invited or pushed to account for their ATR-involvement,

Malawian Christians will give unproblematising accounts whereby they can condone ATR-involvement. They make clear that they place ATR at a different level than Christianity. Their involvement in Christianity is principled, structural and most important. Their ATR–involvement is incidental and not out of intrinsic motivation.

The way in which Malawian Christians account for ATR shows that they are able to skillfully tune their verbal actions to the actions of their conversation-partner, and to an imaginary audience, which they expect to look over the interviewer's shoulder.

This research demonstrates that labels like syncretism, religious pluralism or 'African Christianity' do not adequately reflect Malawians' religious practices. As suggested in the introduction, by using these labels one imposes a too coherent order from above is imposed and an artificial congruity between Christianity and ATR is created. Analysis of Malawian Christians' discourse about ATR and dual religious involvement made clear that Christians can separate performing certain ATR-practices and –beliefs from carrying out a Christian identity-project, and do not consider the two as obstructing each other. Thus, unlike some scholars suggest, Malawian Christians don't appear to suffer from moral and mental confusion or religious schizophrenia. In some sense Chakanza (1998) is right when he says that Malawian Christians lead dualistic lives. But they do this in a skilful and unproblematic way.

In the outline of the church-policy in chapter 4 it was mentioned that most Malawian Christians don't express to feel any need for inculturation or even straightforwardly disapprove of this policy of the Roman Catholic Church. The respondent's disapproval of the inculturation-policy can be understood now. This attempt of theologians and progressive clergy to bring ATR into Christianity is the purposeful, structural and on principle kind of combining of the two religions ATR and Christianity, which normally Malawian Christians disapprove of. Carrying out a policy of inculturation implies to attend to ATR and Christianity as two things –two religions- of the same order, and to strive for bringing them closer to each other, placing them almost at the same level. This is exactly what the Malawian Christians respondents problematise, as we have seen in the interview-extracts.

In the outline of the church-policy it has been mentioned as well that clergy regularly ignore ATR-practices. It was suggested that they had no other option, as, although the missionaries started to make Malawians forsake their indigenous religions, Malawians persistently hang on to their

ATR-practices and beliefs. However, now insight has been gained in the patterns of Malawian Christian's accounting, the clergy's condoning of ATR-practices and –beliefs can be explained differently. Clergy can justifiably accept that mothers give their children a necklace as part of a birth ritual, as long as they do make clear that they should not bring these children in church. By keeping ATR outside the church they divorce ATR and Christianity. Thus, although they condone Christians' ATR-involvement, they do adhere to the claim that Christianity and ATR cannot go together.

It can be concluded that Malawian Christians distinguish the having of certain ATR-'beliefs' and performing of certain ATR-practices as Christian, from the religious 'syncretism' which the churches, and they themselves, condemn. 'Indeed, I do visit idols, I consult inspired men and soothsayers, but I don't leave the church of God. I am a Catholic.' is something a contemporary Malawian Christian could have said as well. And, if someone would rebuke Malawian Christians for dealing with ATR as Christian they could answer 'they wouldn't have done so if anyone had told them it was wrong.' Although telling it is wrong probably does not make a difference. It can be expected that Malawian Christians will continue for a long time to acknowledge the existence of witchcraft and ancestral spirits, and therefore to perform certain ATR-practices. Analysis of Malawian Christians' discourse has shown that it is hardly possible, and moreover not necessary, for devoted Malawian Christians to forsake their ATR. It can be expected that, like in Europe of the fourth to eight century after Christ, Christianity and what can be called 'African traditional religion' will continue to coexist for a while. Or rather, Malawian Christians will continue to be committed to Christianity and perform certain traditional practices or have certain traditional 'beliefs'. Malawian Christians are skilful members who can meet the dual social demand, which the coercive omnipresent ATR-reality and Christianity bring along. Malawian Christians can attend to and construct ATR-'beliefs' as real, justify their ATR-involvement, and at the same time they can show to be devoted Christians who are committed to Christianity and its laws, which state that ATR and Christianity 'can not go together'.

7. 2 Final comments and recommendations

Some final comments and suggestions for further research can be made. The interviews have been carried out in English, which is not the Malawian respondents', or the interviewer's native language. The extracts show that although respondents speak English rather well, there are some misunderstandings. One can question to which extent 'talk' can be fruitfully analysed from a discourse analytic perspective if the people who are producing this discourse cannot fully express themselves, or don't fully understand each other. However, although communication-problems made some extracts useless for analysis, most parts of the interviews were understandable enough to analyse. Talk does not become less interesting when conversation-partners are restricted in their abilities of expression. If people don't speak the language fluently, they will still engage in all kinds of action. They will still produce meaningful worlds and particular versions of reality. One may argue that as both the interviewer and the respondents are no native speakers, there is an increased risk that the researcher misinterprets what respondents says and therefore misinterprets the function' of their assertions. However, there is always a risk for miscommunication, also between native speakers. Moreover, in this research discursive actions have been identified on the basis of a large amount of interview-extracts, a collection of accounts, which appeared to follow a certain pattern. Hence, the researcher would have to misinterpret many extracts in order to endanger the validity of the claims made in this study. Moreover, extracts and their analysis have been critically discussed with fellow-researchers as well, and their interpretations of what was said and done in the extracts have been taken into account. This increases the reliability of assertions about Malawian Christian's discursive actions.

Another comment pertains the use of the label 'ATR' in this study. This study has investigated how Christian Malawians talk about involvement in Christianity and in practices and beliefs, which are declared to belong to ATR. However, one can question whether it is justified to lump together this variety of practices and 'beliefs' under the denominator 'African Traditional Religion'. Not only because certain ATR-aspects differ quite a lot from each other, but one can also argue whether it is correct to call them *religious* practices and beliefs. Especially initiation is a rather secular practice, which has more an educating than a religious function. However, using ATR as general label for different practices and beliefs does make some sense as the practices and beliefs, which are said to belong to ATR, have several things in common. For example, especially in the past the church denounced them all as 'pagan' and, on the whole, the church still disapproves of them. Thus they were all declared in some way as opposites to the other religion: Christianity. Also the fact that no distinction was made in this study between initiation rites and other ATR-practices seems justified as the church rejects initiations as least as much as other more religious ATR-aspects, and because Malawians hang on to this practices at least as much as to others. And, most importantly, Malawian Christians accounted for initiations in the same way as for other ATR-aspects. They used the same problematising and unproblematsing accounts. Nevertheless, as this study made clear, one should be very careful to see ATR as a religion like Christianity. This does not do justice to the way in which Malawians themselves orient to ATR-practices and -'beliefs'. A phrase like 'religious tradition' instead of 'religion' seems to reflect the way in which Malawian Christians attend to ATR-practices and –beliefs somewhat better.

Some recommendations for future research can be made. The possibility of differences between the various ATR-practices and beliefs suggests that it will be useful in future research to focus on specific practices or 'beliefs' instead of ATR in general. This will give the opportunity to investigate into more detail the dynamics in talk pertaining these specific aspects, and to see whether accounting-patterns differ per practice or 'belief' or not.

This study identified different kinds of 'talk' which Christian Malawians engage in: ideological 'identity talk' and pragmatic 'practical talk'. Further conversational analytic research could reveal more precisely how and when Christian Malawians exactly switch between the different kinds of discourses.

Another interesting follow-up study would be to focus on some special groups who can be expected to be highly involved in ATR, like traditional healers or people who are said to be witches. In general, 'witchcraft' itself is a relevant topic for further research. This research has shown how omnipresent, and taken for granted the reality of witches and witchcraft is. Witchcraft permeates, in a negative way, in all kinds of Malawian Christians' daily practices. As witchcraft seems to turn on jealousy, it might impede especially ambitious and successful people. Fear to reach prosperity is not exactly what a poor developmental country like Malawi can use. Thus, insight in witchcraft and how it works in African societies like Malawi can be of importance for several developmental-issues as well.

List of references

Antaki, C. & Widdicombe, S. (Eds.). (1998). *Identities in talk.* London: Sage.
Baerveldt, C. (1999). *Culture and the consensual coordination of actions.* Unpublished doctoral dissertation, KUN, Nijmegen.
Baerveldt, C. & Verheggen, Th. (1999). Enactivism and the experiential reality of culture: Rethinking the epistemological basis of cultural psychology. *Culture & Psychology, 5(2),* 183-206.
Baerveldt, C. & Voestermans, P. (2000). Het misverstand cultuur: Naar een psychologie van biculturaliteit. [The misunderstanding of culture: Towards a psychology of biculturality]. *Nederlands Tijdschrift voor de Psychologie, 55,* 109-120.
Binsbergen, W. M. J. (1981). in *Zambia Religious change*: Exploratory studies. London: Kegan Paul International.
Bourdieu, P. (1990). *In other words: Essays towards a reflexive sociology.* Cambridge: Polity Press.
Chakanza, J. C. (1998). Unfinished agenda: Puberty rites and the response of the Roman Catholic Church in Southern Malawi, 1901-1994. In J. Cox (ed.), *Rites of passage in contemporary Africa.* Cardiff: Academic Press.
Chingota, F. L. (1995). An historical account of the attitude of Blantyre Synod of the Church of Central Africa Presbyterian towards initiation rites. *Religion in Malawi,* 5, 8-13.
Dijk, R. van (1989). Cultuur als excuus voor falende hulpverlening. [culture as excuse for failing health-services] *Medische Antropologie* 1 (2), 131-143
Dierick, G. (1983). Een pinguïn in de savanne? Missie en ontwikkeling in oost-Afrika ter discussie. [A pinguïn in the savanne? Discussing mission and development in East-Africa] In Schoffelleers, J. M., Obdeijn, H., Schoenaker, H., Trouwborst, A., Wolf, J. J., de, Amelsfoort, V. van, Heijke, J., Doornbos, M. R., Bergen, van, J. P., Dierick, G. (Eds.), *Missie en ontwikkeling in Oost-Afrika.* Nijmegen: KSC.
Droogers, A. (1989). Syncretism: The problem of definition, the definition of the problem. In Gort, J. D., Vroom, M. H., Fernhout, R., & Wessels, A. (Eds.), *Dialogue and syncretism: An interdisciplinary approach.*, Grand Rapids: Eerdmans.

Edwards, D. (1995). A commentary on discursive and cultural psychology. *Culture & Psychology, 55-65.*
Fabian, J. (1985). Religious pluralism: An ethnographic approach. In Binsbergen, van., W.& M., Schoffeleers, M. (Eds.) Theoretical explorations in African religion.
Garfinkel, H. (1967) *Studies in Ethnomethodology.* Englewood Cliffs, N.J.: Prentice-Hall
Have, P. ten (1999a). *Doing conversation analysis: A practical guide.* London: Sage.
Have, P. ten. (1999b). De probleemstelling in kwalitatief sociologisch onderzoek [The research question in qualitative sociological research] (online). Available: http://www. pscw.uva.nl/emca/PS.htm
Have, P., ten (1999c). Kwalitatief sociologisch onderzoek [Qualitative Sociological Research] (online). Available: http://www. pscw.uva.nl/emca/KSO.htm
Have, P. ten (1990d) 'Methodological issues in conversation analysis', *Bulletin de Méthodologie Sociologique,* 27 23-51 [ook online http://www.pscw.uva.nl// emca/mica.htm
Jong, A. H. de (1994). *Missie op een keerpunt in de context van Oost-Afrika. De rol van Nederlandse missionarissen in het politieke en kerkelijke opvoedingsproces in Tanzania, Kenya, Uganda en Malawi 1945-1975.* [Mission on a moment of change in the context of East-Africa. The role which Dutch missionaries played in the political and ecclesiastical rearing-process]. Berg en Dal:
Katani, A. M. (1999) Birth rituals among the Chewa of Traditional Authority Kawamba in Kasungu district and the attitude of the church of Central Africa Presbyterian (CCAP) Nkhoma Synod. Unpublished Bachelor's thesis, University of Malawi, Zomba.
Kiernan, J. (1994). *Variation on a Christian theme: The healing synthesis of Zulu Zionism.* In C. Stewart, & R. Shaw (Eds.), *Syncretism / anti-syncretism: The politics of religious synthesis* (pp. 69-84). London: Routledge
Kuppen, J.J.M (1992). They discovered the wonders of God in their culture: mortuary rites and inculturation in Malawi. Unpublished master's thesis, Katholieke Univeristeit Nijmegen, Nijmegen
MacMullen, R. (1997). *Christianity and paganism in the fourth to eight centuries.* New Haven: Yale University Press.
Mbiti, J.S. (1969). *African religions and philosophy.* London: Heinemann

Meyer, B. (1994). Beyond syncretism: translation and diabolization in the appropriation of Protestantism in Africa. In C. Stewart, & R. Shaw (Eds.), *Syncretism/anti-syncretism: The politics of religious synthesis* (pp. 45-68). London: Routledge

Moerman, M. (1988). *Talking culture*. Philadelphia: University of Pennsylvania Press.

National Statistical Office (1998). Press release: 1998 Malawi Population and housing census final results. (online). Available: http//www.nso.malawi.net/

Potter, J., & Wetherell, M. (1987). *Discourse and social psychology*. Newbury Park, CA: Sage.

Ott, M. (2000). *Research proposal: Popular Christianity in Malawi: An empirical-systematic approach.* Unpublished manuscript, Kachere Institute for Research on Religion, Culture and Society.

Schoffeleers, J. M. (1983). Het Christendom in Afrika. [Christianity in Africa]. In Schoffelleers et al, (Eds.), *Missie en ontwikkeling in Oost-Afrika*. Nijmegen: KSC.

Shotter, J. & Gergen, K. (1989). *Texts of identity*. London: Sage.

Stewart, C., & Shaw, R. (1994). Introduction: Problematising syncretism. In C. Stewart, & R. Shaw (Eds.), *Syncretism / anti-syncretism: The politics of religious synthesis* (pp. 1- 26). London: Routledge.

Tengatenga, J. (1998). Religious pluralism in Malawi: A challenge to the church. *Religion in Malawi, 8,* 16-23.

Turner, H. W. (1979b). *Religious innovation in Africa: Collected essays on new religious movements,* Boston, Mass.: G. K. Hall.

Wendroff, A. P. (1985). Trouble-shooters and trouble-makers: Witchfinding and traditional Malawian medicine. PhD, City University of New York

Warkentin, R. (1996), Traditional African religion and modern Christianity in Zaire: The case of the Bira. *Anthropologica, 38,* 3-19.

Wittgenstein, L. (1953/1958). *Philosophical Investigations*, Trans. G. E. M., Anscombe, Oxford, Blackwell.

Worldbank (1998). *World development report 1998*, New York: OUP.

World health organisation/UNAIDS (1998). Epidemiological fact sheet on HIV/AIDS and sexually transmitted diseases: Malawi. (online). Available: http://www.unaids.org/hivaidsinfo.

Zweerden, E. van der. (1994). Sovjet philosophy –The ideology and the handmade. A historical and critical analysis of Sovjet philosophy, with a case study into Sovjet history of philosophy. Enschede Copywright 2000

Appendix A. Respondents' characteristics

Table 1. Respondents' characteristics

Respondent	Sex	Age	Ethnicity	Domicile	Education	Religion	Remarks
1. Mr. O	M	36	Chewa/-Tumbuka	Town/village[2]	Secondary school	CCAP	Church-deacon
2. Mr. Jo	M	26	Nyanga	Village	Secondary school (JC, almost MC)	CCAP	
3. Mr. F	M	40	Lomwe	Village	Sec. school	RC	
4. Rev. Ku	M	49	Ngoni	Town/village	Sec. school +[3]	CCAP	
5. Mrs. L	F	64	Yao	Village	Primary school +	CCAP	
6. Mrs. J	F	49	Yao	Village	Primary school	CCAP	
7. Mr. Ka	M	59	Yao	Village	Sec. school	CCAP	Church elder and village headman
8. Mr. Ja	M	25	Tumbuka	Town	University	RC	
9. Mr. S	M	18	Lomwe	Town	Sec. school	RC	
10. Mrs. T	F	16	Tonga	Town	Sec. school	CCAP	
11. Mrs. A	F	38	Chewa/Yao	Town	Sec. school +	CCAP	
12. Mr. H	M	40	Lomwe	Village/town	Sec. school+	RC	
13. Mr. M	M	54	Lomwe	Village	Sec. school-[4]	RC (before Jehovah's Witness)	
14. Mrs. G	F	43	Tonga	Town	Primary school	Old Apostolic Church	Born in South-Africa, came to Malawi at 14 years

Ad 1. "Chewa/Tumbuka" means that respondent could not identify him- or herself with one ethnic group.

Ad 2. "Town/village" means that respondent has been living both in town and village.

Ad 3. "Sec. school" means that respondent did some additional courses after secondary school.

Ad 4. "Secondary school" means that respondent almost passed the secondary school exam.

Appendix D: Transcription Notation

(.)	short pause
(0.3)	timed pause of .3 second
(word?)	transcriber's guess at an unclear part of the tape
( )	unclear speech
run= =on	'leaching' , 'equal' signs link material that runs on,
lo:ng	colons show stretched sound
under	underlining indicated emphasis
CAPITALS	indicate speech louder than that surrounding it
° soft °	degree signs indicate speech spoken more quietly than surrounding talk.
>fast<	talk which is produced quicker than surrounding talk
over[lap [overlap	square brackets denote the start of overlapping talk
[ ] or (…)	indicates that material has been left out of the extract
[text]	researcher's remarks

Appendix B.

Involvement in ATR per Respondent, per Practice

Table 2. Involvement in ATR: alleged practices and beliefs per respondent

Respondent	Initiation		Traditional healing			Raincalling		Traditional funeral	Birth ritual		Witchcraft		Ancestral Spirits		Total
	Self	Children	Use trad. medicine	Herbalist	Witch-doc	Pray Ancestors	Rain-withholding		self	Children	Real	Belief	Real	Belief	
1. Mr. O	-	-	+	-	-	-			-	+	+	-			3
2. Mr. Jo	+		+	+	+	-	-	+			+		+	-	7
3. Mr F.	-	-		?	?						+		+	-	2
4. Rev Ku	-					-	-				+		+	-	2
5. Mrs. L	+	-		-	-	-			-		+?	-	-		2

	+	−	+	−	+	−	+	−	+	−	+	−	+	−	Total
6. Mrs. J	+	−			−	−	−				+		+?	−	−	3
7. Rev. Ka	−	−	+		+	−	−	−	−		+	−	+		+	−	5
8. Mr. Ja	−	−	+		+	+?	−		+		+		+		+	+	8
9. Mr. S	−	−	+		+	+	−		+		+		+		+	−	6
10. Mrs. T	−	−	−	−	−	−	−		−	−	+?	−	?	−	1
11. Mrs. A	+	−	+	−	−	−	?		+	?	−	+			4
12. Mr. H	−	−	+		+	+	−		−		+		+		+		6
13. Mr. M	+	+	+		+		−			+	+	+		+		8
14. Mrs. G	−	−	+		+		−	?	+	−	−	+	−		−	4
Total	5	1	9	8	3	−	2 (+2 doubt)	6	2 (+1 doubt)	2	14	−	9	−	

NB:
- \+ means respondent asserts to have practised/ to believe in
- − means respondent asserts *not* to have practised/ *not* to believe in
- ? means respondent expresses doubts whether he/she believes in, doubts the "reality" of a belief or doubts whether he/she will perform practice in future.
- empty cell means topic has not been discussed/ involvement doesn't become clear from data

Appendix C. Malawi in Short

Malawi is the setting of this research. Data have been collected in Malawi, respondents are Malawians and have all been living most of their time in this "warm heart of Africa". Some geographic, historical and demographic facts of Malawi will be portrayed here. Unless stated otherwise, data are from 1998. Sources are the 1998 Malawi Population and Housing Census of Malawi's National Statistical Office and the World Development Report of the worldbank. To be able to place the numbers in perspective, some comparative data about Holland are provided as well. Data about the Dutch situation pertain the year 2000, source is 'Centraal Bureau voor Statistiek'.

Table 3. Demographic and economic facts about Malawi

1.Population	10 million
2.Population Density	105 per km^2
3.Urban Population	14 %
4.Rural Population	86 %
5.Literacy rates	58% (town 79%, village 54 %; men 64%, women 51 %)
6.Crude Birth Rate	37,9
7.Fertility Rate	6,8 (Netherlands: 1,54)
8.Crude Death Rate	21,1 (Netherlands: 9,4)
9.Under Five Mortality	189 (Netherlands 0,5)
10.Life Expectancy	39 (Netherlands: 76)
11. Access to (western) health care	81 % (urban population), 29% (rural population)
12.GDP	1,7 billion (US $)
13.HDI[1]	159 (Netherlands: 7)

Ad 5. Literacy rates: percentage of the population above five years who can read or write in at least one language.
Ad 6. Crude Birth Rate: number of births per 1000 people
Ad 8. Crude Death Rate: number of deaths per 1000 people
Ad 9. Under Five Mortality: number of deaths of children under five, per 1000 children born alive.

Ad 10. Life Expectancy: expected years to live at birth. Life expectancy in Malawi has been declining from 46 in 1979 to 39 in 1998. The aids-epidemic is probably one of the causes for this decrease in life expectancy.
Ad 11. Source: WHO/UNAIDS. Notice the large discrepancy between the rural and urban population whereas far out the largest part of Malawian population lives in rural areas.
Ad 12. GDP: Gross Domestic Product in billion US-dollars
Ad 13. HDI: Human Development Index. This is a measurement of human development, measured by life expectancy, educational attainment and adjusted income. The HDI has 174 'ranks', rank 1 is the most, 174 least 'developed' country.

Table 4. Facts about Malawi: Miscellaneous

Discovered by Europeans in:	End of sixteenth century, by Portuguese. 'Rediscovered' in 1859 by David Livingstone
Arrival mission:	1861 (Anglican), 1875 (Free Church of Schotland and Church of Scotland), 1889 (Dutch Reformed Church), 1901 (Roman Catholics). In 1924/26 three protestant churches merged into the Church Central of Africa Presbyterian
Colonised in:	1891
Coloniser:	Great Britain
Colonial name:	Nyasaland
Gained independence:	1964
Political Situation:	Since 1994: Democracy: Before: Dictatorial
President:	Mr. Muluzi
	Before 1994: Dr. H.K Banda, 'President for life'
Ethnicities:	Several, some of the largest: Chewa, Tumbuka, Tonga, Nyanga, Lomwe, Yao, Ngoni
Official Languages:	English, Chichewa
	Most ethnicities also have their own languages

Appendix E: Interview Schedule

Respondents were posed a selection of the questions portrayed here.

Introduction

Before we start with the interview I would like to say some things about my self, my research and the procedure of this interview. First of all I want to say that everything which you tell me during this interview will be kept strictly confidential. I will write down what you told me, but it will be anonymous. I will not write down your name on your story. Nobody can see that it was you who said the things which are said in this interview.

> However, I would like to ask if it is alright with you if I would rec??ord this interview on tape. I think you can tell me a lot of interesting things for my research. If I don't record it I am afraid I might forget some things. If you want to I can delete the tape-recording after I wrote the interview down.
> Is it all right with you if I record our conversation on tape?
> Do you want me to delete the tape-recording after I processed the interview-data? (if no objection to recording).
> My supervisors in Holland and a few fellow-students of mine might be interested in hearing some parts of this interview. Do you mind if they would hear this interview?
> I will tell something more about myself and my research now. I study psychology of culture and religion in Holland. I came to Malawi for six months for my graduation-research, to finish my study. It's difficult to explain what my research is exactly about; I can explain it better at the end of the interview. At the moment I can say I am interested in personal experiences of life in Malawi. I am especially interested in experiences of religion in Malawi. Because you are a Malawian and you speak English, it would be very interesting for me to interview you about your experiences of life in Malawi. I think the interview will take approximately one and a half-hour. Is this all right with you?
> Here I have a list with questions which I will pose one after another. You only have to tell me what you yourself think or feel. I am

- merely interested in your own personal opinion and your own experiences. So there are definitely no 'correct' or 'wrong' answers.
- Maybe sometimes you don't understand what I mean during the interview, then just tell me. Ill try to make my self more clear then. I will ask questions as well if I don't understand something you're saying okay?
- The questions might be rather personal. Of course you don't have to answer a question if you don't want.
- If during the interview you say something and afterwards you realise you don't want it to be on tape, just tell me. I can delete that part of the recording then.
- I would like to make some notes during our conversation. This is only to help me to remember things during the interview. I will not show the notes to other persons. Is it all right with you if I make notes during the interview?
- This was what I wanted to say before our interview. Do you have any questions or remarks at this moment? Okay, then I would like to start with the first question.

I) Biographical data:

(I'll ask for the name but will emphasise that's just for making the conversation easier and that I will delete the name afterwards)
1. Male/female
2. What's your name?
3. How old are you?
4. Where do you live?
5. Since how long have you been living here? Where were you born?
6. What kind of education did you have?
7. What's your profession, what kind of work do you do?
8. Can you tell me something about your family? (brothers/sisters, parents - domicile/education/profession/ religious affiliation?
9. Have your parents been Christians their entire life? (if no:)
10. Do you know when and why they became Christians?

II) Bireligiosit

2.1 Identity & ethnic-group
1. To which ethnic-group do you belong? Are you a Tumbuka, Yao, Chewa

or...
2. Why do you call yourself a ... what makes you a .....?
3. Can you tell me what being ....means to you? Is it important for you? Do you feel different from Malawians who belong to other ethnic groups? Why/ why not?

2.2 Identity & Problem-solving practices

NB: with all these questions I'll be alert on answers which point to the influence of either Christianity or ATR, and question further when this issue is mentioned, trying to find out if 'bireligious'-conflicts are perceived/experienced.

Puberty /Initiation

1. I understood most ethnic-groups in Malawi have initiation rites. Your ethnic-group as well?
2. Would you say it is important that there are initiation rites and that children go to them? Why/why not?
3. Did you undergo initiation rites yourself? Why/why not?
4. (if yes) Can you tell me what it means for you to be initiated? Were they important to you? In what sense? What would have been different if you had not been initiated?
5. Do you see yourself as different from other ...who did/did not attend these initiation rites? In what sense?
6. Do you ever regret you aren't initiated sometimes maybe or are you happy?
7. Were your children initiated, or would you want your children to be initiated?
8. I understood sometimes clergy of some Christian churches don't want people to go to initiation rites. What do you think about that? Do you understand those leaders of Christian churches? Do you agree with them? Why/why not?
9. Do you know what the opinion of the clergy of your church is about these initiation rites? What do you think about that opinion?
10. If your church forbids you to attend traditional initiation rites, would you still send your children to those rites? Why?
11. I understood some churches have designed their own Christian-initiation

rites. Do you know them?
12. If you would have to choose between either going to/sending your children to a Christian-initiation or to a ......initiation, or to none at all, what would you choose? Why?
13. I understood some people send their children to initiation rites although their church is opposed to them. What do you think about that? Why do you think they send their children to them?

Disease

1. Can you remember a time you were quite ill in your life? For example the last time you have been ill, can I ask you what kind of illness did you have?
2. What did you do to become better?
3. Did you go to some kind of traditional healer?
4. (if yes:) What kind of traditional healer was it, what did he do? Were some kind of divine powers involved, in some way?
5. Did it help?
6. Can you tell me why you went to the traditional healer? Why do you think it helped?
7. Did you go to the doctor as well when you were sick? Why/why not?
8. (if no to q 3:) Why not? Did you go to a doctor or to hospital?
9. Why did you go to the doctor and not to the traditional healer, or why trad.healer and no doctor?
10. Have there been other times during your life in which you were ill and you did go to a traditional healer?
11. If you become seriously ill in the future, do you think you would go to a traditional healer or to a doctor? Why?
12. If you were ill and went to a western-doctor but wouldn't become better, would you go and see a traditional healer?
13. If you went to a traditional healer but wouldn't become better, would you go and see a doctor?
14. Are there certain situations when you would not go to a traditional healer? For example in case of certain illnesses? Like Aids? Infertility? Or any other situation? Or not to a western doctor?
15. (if said not going to trad.healers) What do you think of people who do go to traditional healers, (distinguish between trad.helalers who use super. powers and those who don't) do you understand them, or do you think they shouldn't? Why?

16. Or are there perhaps certain types of persons for whom traditional healers are better then doctors to other types? Certain ethnic groups? Religion?
13. Did you happen to ask God in some way for help when you were ill? How? Would you pray, go to church?
14. Maybe this is a difficult question but what did you expect God would do; support you, cure the illness?
15. 19.   (if not experienced illness) Do you think you will ask God for help if you become seriously ill in the future How? Would you pray, go to church? What would you expect from God, or what would you hope he would do ? Cure the illness?
20. Do you know what your church thinks about going to a trad.healer? What do you think about that opinion?
21. (If said both going to trad.healer in which case certain 'divine' powers were involved & praying to God). If your church, would forbid you to go to trad.healers would you not go anymore? Why/ why not
22. Imagine your sister is ill. She goes to a traditional healer who says he uses supernatural powers to cure the diseases. She also prays to God for help. What would you think about that? Would it change anything about her being Christian/ Christian faith?
23 If someone would say to you you shouldn't both go to a trad.healer and pray to God, because then you are asking help from other divine powers or spirits then God. In the bible it is said that one should not abide other Gods then the Christian God. What would you say to him/her?

Death

1. I would like to talk with you about a rather sad subject now; about death and funerals. I understood that often in funerals in Malawi there are traditional elements which belong to the ethnic-group of the dead person. So many times people are buried for example according to certain customs in their own ethnic group. For example at Chewa funerals there will be Nyau-dancers present, or people cut their hair after the funeral.
2. Have these kinds of elements also been in funerals of people you know, like friends or relatives?
3. (If yes) Were they Christians?
4. Maybe this is a strange question, but if you yourself are going to die, do you want this kind of trad. elements in your funeral? What kind of? Why?
5. Do you want your funeral to be a Christian funeral? What would for example make the funeral Christian to you? Why?

6. Can you see traditional elements as well in funerals of Christians?
7. What do you think about it when a Christian has trad. elements in his/her funeral? Does it make any difference for their being Christian? In what sense? Logical?
8. If you would have to choose between.... elements and Christian elements in your funeral, it is not possible to have them both in it. What would you choose? Why?
9. Do you know what the opinion of your church is about ... elements in funerals of followers of their church?
10. If the leaders of your church would say you're not allowed to put ... elements in your funeral, would you leave them out? Or would you still want ... elements in your funeral? Why, why not?
11. (If not)Can you imagine some people want a funeral with ..... elements even though their clergy disapprove of it? Why/Why not?

Natural disaster

1. I understood that this year the rain-season started very late, in October and November not enough rain had fallen for the time of year. Maybe this is a strange question, but can you tell me what you thought or felt at that time? For example were you surprised, or worried, or do you think like okay, I am sure it will be raining soon?
2. In such a situation of drought, do you want to do something about it? Did you have any ideas what you could do about it?
3. Do you have any ideas about the reasons for such a period? Why would you think such a period occurred?
4. I understood there are certain more traditional practices that are sometimes performed during droughts. Do or did you perform those practices yourself? Why/why not?
5. Do you know people who perform?
6. What's your opinion about their performing of these practices?
7. Imagine your sister/brother is Christian and performs those practices. What do you think about that? Does it make him/her a different Christian? Does it change anything about his/her Christian faith?
8. (if said performing traditional practices) If you would have to choose between praying to God or to ancestors for rain; what would you choose?

Birth

1. (if talking to father/mother)

When your child(ren) were born, were certain rites performed after birth, at a certain moment? (if yes)
2. What kind of? Can you explain to me why those rites were performed?
3. Why/why not?
4. Was the/your child baptised in a Christian church? Why did you want/do you know why they wanted it to be baptised?
5. Do you know what your church thinks about those birth-rites? What do you think about that opinion?
6. (If not talking to father/mother) I understood some people in Malawi do special things when a child is born, perform certain birth-rites. Do you know of those rites?
7. When you were born, do you now whether those rites were performed for you?
8. Are you glad they were performed, or not?
9. Were you baptised? Glad/not glad?
10. If you would have a child would you want the birth-rites to be performed for him? Why/why not?
11. Would you also make sure that your child was baptised? Why?
12. Can people, according to you, both perform birth-rituals and let their child being baptized?
13. Some people say it's in a way doing the same thing twice. Do you agree? Why/why not?
14. If you would have to choose between letting your child being baptised and performing birth-rituals, what would you choose? Why?
15. What do you think about Christians who perform traditional birth-rites?

Spirit possession/ancestral spirits

1. Do you believe in the existance of ancestral spirits? Maybe this is a difficult question but why/why not? Did you have any experiences with them?
2. I heard that sometimes people in Malawi can become possessed by spirits. Is that true, can that happen? Did you have any experiences with this?
3. Some people told me that here in Malawi people can bewitch each other. Do you think that's true, can that actually happen? Why/why not? Experiences?
4. (if said both believing in Christian god and ancestral spirits/witchcraft) I think that according to some people it's strange to believe both in God and in ancestral spirits or witchcraft. They would for example say both

ancestral spirits and witchcraft have to do with supernatural powers which are not mentioned in the Bible. Do you think yourself it's strange to believe in both ancestral spirits, witchcraft and the Christian God? Why/why not?
5. (if belief both in ancestral spirits and God) If someone would say to you you should not believe in ancestral spirits because the bible says that one is not allowed to abide other Gods then the Christian God. How would you react, what would you answer?

III. Christianity

1. Perhaps this a difficult question, but can you tell me what being Christian means to you? Would you say it influences your daily life? In what way?

IV. Interaction Christianity/ indigenous religion/identity

1. If someone wants to get to know you; would you find it more important that this person knows you are ....(religious affiliation) or that you are ....(ethnic group)?
2. You are a Christian. You are also ... Do you perhaps sometimes experience any problems being both a real Christian and a real ...? For example I can imagine you'd like to perform...practices which you are not allowed to perform because of your church-membership?
3. We've been talking about some traditional ... practices like....Are .....who perform those practices different from .... who don't?.
4. You said you performed...... You also go to church. I was wondering, I don't know but, do you perhaps sometimes think about the performing of these two things ? Do you for example start thinking about it why you are doing it both, or do you realise that you are glad that you are able to do it both?
5. Sometimes elements of indigenous religions, or traditional practices, can be seen in Christian practices in Malawi. For example certain rites or symbols from African traditional religion might be introduced in the Christian mass. What do you think about that? Do you like it, or not,
6. I would like to give an example (give example Catholic father who combines baptism with birth ritual.) What do you think about that?

www.ingramcontent.com/pod-product-compliance
Lightning Source LLC
Chambersburg PA
CBHW031713230426
43668CB00006B/200